Handbook
of
Photography

Handbook
of
Photography

Ronald P. Lovell

Fred C. Zwahlen, Jr.

James A. Folts

Oregon State University
Corvallis, Oregon

Delmar Publishers

an International Thomson Publishing company I(T)P®

Albany • Bonn • Boston • Cincinnati • Detroit • London • Madrid
Melbourne • Mexico City • New York • Pacific Grove • Paris • San Francisco
Singapore • Tokyo • Toronto • Washington

This book is dedicated to all photographers—past, present, and future: Click away!

Cover photographs (clockwise from upper left) by Dorothea Lange, Neil Armstrong, Smithsonian Institution, and Lewis Hine.
Interior photographs not otherwise credited were by James Folts, Chris Johns, Keith Peterson, Randy Wood, and Fred Zwahlen

Delmar Staff
Senior Administrative Editor: John Anderson
Developmental Editor: Michelle Ruelos Cannistraci
Production Manager: Larry Main
Art and Design Coordinator: Nicole Reamer
Cover design: Mick Brady
Text design: Liz Kingslien

For information, address Delmar Publishers Inc.
3 Columbia Circle, Box 15-015
Albany, New York 12212

Library of Congress Cataloging-in-Publication Data

Lovell, Ronald P.
    Handbook of photography / Ronald P. Lovell, Fred C. Zwahlen, Jr.,
  James A. Folts.—4th ed.
        p.   cm.
    Includes bibliographical references and index.
    ISBN 0-8273-7913-7
      1. Photography—Handbooks, manuals, etc.   I. Zwahlen, Fred C., 1924- .
II. Folts, James A.   III. Title.
TR146.l67   1998
770—dc21   96-29942
                                              CIP

Contents

PART ONE

Cameras and Picture Taking

Chapter One: The Camera

PART TWO

Developing and Printing

Part Three

Handling Light and Color

PART FOUR

Digital Photography

PART FIVE

Professional Issues in Photography

Chapter Thirteen: Photography, Ethics, and the Law

Chapter Fourteen: Careers in Photography

PART SIX

Photo History

Chapter Fifteen: A Short History of Photography

Preface

THE FIRST THREE EDITIONS of this book aimed to teach those who had never before held a camera how to take photographs, develop film, and make prints. To achieve that goal, we devoted a chapter to each basic step in the photographic process—from focusing the camera on the person or object to be photographed to the emergence of the final picture, mounted for display or ready for use in print.

Now, four years after the publication of the third edition, the experience of thousands of beginning photography students tells us that the book achieved its goal. For the fourth edition, the best-selling approach and format of the first three editions have been retained. We have added several chapters on the important new field of digital photography, as well as updated material on film, equipment, and technique. In addition, a number of new photos are included in this edition, many by noted photographers of the past and present. These will provide both inspiration and valuable information on techniques to beginning photographers.

Handbook of Photography, fourth edition, attempts to cover its topics in as simple a way as possible. Throughout the book, we encourage readers to recognize that things do go wrong and to understand how to improve the quality of their work. Too many photography books are filled with beautiful pictures but no failures. We have beautiful photographs in our book. But we also have some bad photographs in "What Can Go Wrong?" sections that appear at ends of the technique chapters. Along with the failures shown in these sections are suggestions on how to correct them.

Our aim is to get readers to start taking pictures almost immediately and to learn by doing. To that end, we begin in Chapter 1 with the camera and how it works to record images. In Chapters 2 to 6—the technique chapters—the book takes a "throw-them-in-the-water-to-see-if-they-can-swim-to-shore" approach.

We have chapters on operating the camera, taking the picture, developing film, printmaking, and advanced printmaking. We also explain how to sell your photos. These chapters are unique in that each contains a detailed, how-to-do-it photo essay. Each essay is a simple, but complete step-by-step guide that is intended to help beginners achieve success right from the start.

In Chapters 7, 8, and 9, the book turns to more specialized subjects: lighting, filters, and color photography. The goal of these chapters is to provide a basic understanding of more advanced equipment and techniques. We urge readers to experiment, evaluate, and experiment some more in order to progress to new levels of expertise.

Chapters 10 through 12 provide information on digital photography, from capturing digital images to digital color photography to the digital darkroom.

Chapter 13 discusses the legal rights of photo subjects and photographers. It also covers the moral issues and dilemmas faced by many photographers, especially those involving digital processes. Chapter 14 outlines the many kinds of careers available in photography. The final chapter briefly covers the rich and colorful history of photography.

The final section of the book contains photo assignments, a list of books for additional reading, and a glossary of terms.

Because much of the information in this book is most needed when actually shooting pictures or working in the darkroom, we have designed *Handbook of Photography* to be a portable, accessible reference book as well as a text. Like the previous editions, the fourth edition will fit into a camera bag or the pocket of a parka. The thumb-indexed reference system will quickly lead the user to the needed information. And the book will lie flat, opened to the right page, while both hands are busy with the camera or developing tank.

All of the editions of this book have included a unique feature which we have continued for this one: chapter opening photographs by professional photographers to inspire readers (by their quality) and instruct them (by a brief review of how and why the photograph was taken).

Many people helped in the preparation of all four editions of this book. We thank them now for their continued assistance and support, especially Chris Johns. We appreciate help from the staff members of the various companies, museums, and collections we dealt with for this edition.

Reviews of the fourth edition were provided by Bonnie Ruth Barrett, Northern Arizona University, Flagstaff, Arizona; Cathy Crowell, Cateret Community College, Morehead, North Carolina; Jeffrey N. Curto, College of DuPage, Glen Ellyn, Illinois; Daniel R. Dantonio, Downingtown High School, Downingtown, Pennsylvania; Mark Gonzales, Northern Essex Community College, Haverhill, Massachusetts; Glenn A. Hansen, College of DuPage, Glen Ellyn, Illinois; Victor Lisnyczj, Onondaga Community College, Syracuse, New York;

and Sterling Trantham, New Mexico State University, Las Cruces, New Mexico. We appreciate their constructive advice.

We very much appreciate staff members at Delmar who helped see this fourth edition into print: John Anderson, Michelle Ruelos Cannistraci, Nicole Reamer, Larry Main, and John Fisher. And we thank Mick Brady for the cover design and Liz Kingslien for the text design. We also appreciate the help provided in the early, formative stages of this project by Barbara Riedell, an editor no longer with Delmar.

We are also grateful to the photo teachers and students who used this book in its earlier editions.

With these words of introduction behind us, it is time to get out of the way and let the readers get into the subject that has enticed and enthralled even the most hard-boiled and uncommunicative of people for over 170 years: photography. Whether you are an amateur—with nothing more in mind than taking good photos of the family—or someone who wants to make photography a career, this book is for you. Good luck and happy shooting!

Ron Lovell

Fred Zwahlen

Jim Folts

Cameras

and

Picture

Taking

"As far as I am concerned, taking photographs is a means of understanding which cannot be separated from other means of visual expression. It is a way of shouting, of freeing oneself, not of proving or asserting one's own originality. It is a way of life."

Henri Cartier-Bresson

P · A · R · T

ONE

Cameras and Picture Taking

"As far as I am concerned, taking photographs is a means of understanding which cannot be separated from other means of visual expression. It is a way of shouting, of freeing oneself, not of proving or asserting one's own originality. It is a way of life."

Henri Cartier-Bresson

CHAPTER ONE

THE
Camera

THE
Camera

The Wolcott Mirror Camera, 1840
*(Courtesy, Photographic History Collection,
National Museum of American History, Smithsonian Institution)*

The popularity of daguerreotype portraiture led many entrepreneurs of the day to try to make money on this new development. One of the most innovative camera designs that resulted from this trend was the work of an American manufacturer of dental supplies.

In 1840, Alexander S. Wolcott designed a camera that had no lens. Instead, it used a large, concave mirror at the rear of an oblong box and a daguerreotype plate encased in a frame to capture images. The photographer moved the frame back and forth on a track to focus the image on the plate. The plate faced the mirror. To make an exposure the photographer opened a door on the camera front. The images that resulted from the plate were tiny (about 2 x 2$^1/_2$ inches). Some were as small as a signet ring ($^3/_8$ inches).

Wolcott was not the only dentist to use photography as a sideline. Throughout the 19th century, it was common for dentists to do photographic work in the course of their practices. After all, the often terrified and usually submissive patients already ensconced in the chair made ideal models, however pained they might look.

WITHOUT THE CAMERA, it is safe to say, photographers and photography would not exist. Whether simple or complicated, cheap or expensive, a camera exists to do one thing: to record on film permanent images of the people, places, and things at which it is aimed.

These images vary greatly. They may depict a job or hobby. They may be of planned events or the unexpected. One fact remains, however. Next to the photographer who operates it, the camera is the most indispensable element of photography.

Parts of a Camera

An adjustable camera has seven basic parts: a viewfinder, a focusing mechanism, a shutter, an adjustable aperture, a lens, a body, and devices for holding and advancing film. Figures 1.1, 1.2, and 1.3 show a typical 35 mm camera and its various parts.

- **A viewfinder** allows the photographer to study the subject to be photographed before the picture is taken. The viewfinder offers a preview in miniature of the final image to be produced. Some viewfinders are separate optical devices, often attached to the top of the camera. This position causes a problem

FIGURE 1.1. Front view of 35 mm camera

1. Built-in flash—a flash unit attached to the camera.
2. Mode select buttons—permits setting aperture priority, shutter priority, camera computer program or manual operation.
3. Camera back release—by sliding the release, the camera back can be opened.
4. Lens release button—when depressed, it permits the lens to be removed from the camera body.
5. Focus mode selector—allows the camera to be set on either manual, auto or continuous auto focus.
6. Lens—focuses rays of light to expose the film in the camera.
7. Shutter release button—used to activate shutter so a frame of film can be exposed.
8. Shutter speed dial—permits setting shutter speed either manually, during shutter priority, or by mode selection.

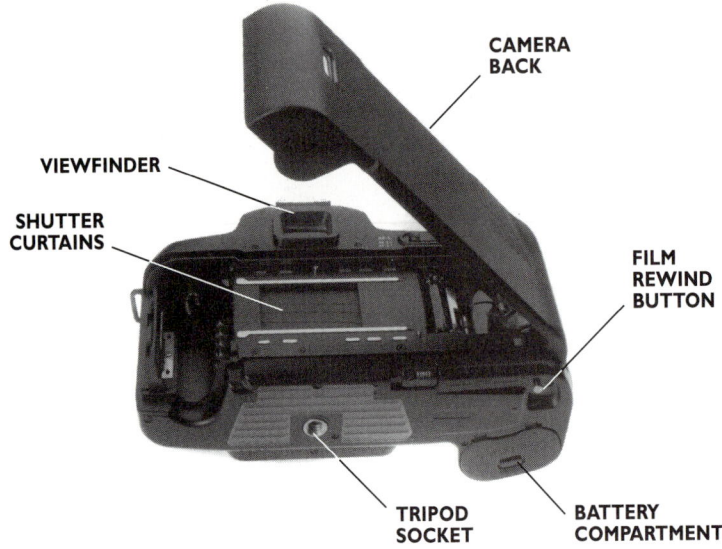

CAMERA BACK

VIEWFINDER

SHUTTER CURTAINS

FILM REWIND BUTTON

TRIPOD SOCKET

BATTERY COMPARTMENT

FIGURE 1.2. Back/bottom view of 35 mm camera

1. Camera back—keeps light from reaching the film and keeps the film flat during exposures.
2. Film rewind button—after pressing it, the film can be rewound from the take-up spool to its original cassette in the film-holding device.
3. Battery compart-ment—houses the battery or batteries necessary to operate the camera.
4. Tripod socket—permits the camera to be placed on a tripod when using a slow shutter speed or when necessary to be exacting when sighting in the area of the viewfinder.
5. Shutter curtains—controls the amount of light reaching the film through the camera lens.
6. Viewfinder—shows the area that will be captured on film.

FIGURE 1.3. Top view of 35 mm camera

1. Focusing ring—makes it possible to view the anticipated photograph in and out of focus.
2. Aperture ring—permits setting the size of the lens opening.
3. Panel display—gives a computerized reading of the camera settings.
4. Accessory shoe—a place where a flash unit can be attached to the camera.
5. Self timer—permits taking a delayed action photograph.

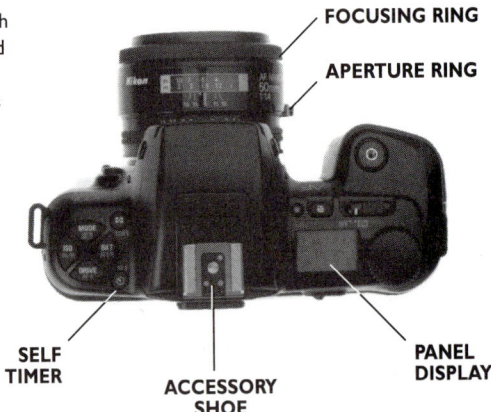

FOCUSING RING

APERTURE RING

SELF TIMER

ACCESSORY SHOE

PANEL DISPLAY

in some simple cameras; because the viewfinder and the lens are located on different planes, they don't see the subject in quite the same way. Accordingly, there is a discrepancy, called the **parallax effect,** between what the lens records on the film and what the eye sees in the viewfinder. This discrepancy is particularly apparent when the camera is close to the subject (Figure 1.4).

In some cameras, the problem is solved by building a parallax correction into the viewfinder system. The viewing system actually tilts as the camera's focusing mechanism is adjusted to compensate for differences in point of view. Other cameras avoid the problem altogether by making the viewfinder and the lens part of the same system. The viewfinder thus looks at the subject from exactly the same point of view as the lens that takes the picture, and parallax is not a factor.

- **A focusing mechanism** moves the lens toward or away from the subject to be photographed and toward or away from the film upon which the image will be recorded. The focusing ring in Figure 1.3 is used to adjust the focusing mechanism. Proper focusing makes the image sharp and distinct; improper focusing makes it blurry and fuzzy.

There are two types of focusing systems: rangefinder and ground-glass viewing screen. In the **rangefinder system,** the photographer sees two images—a direct image through the viewfinder and a reflected image from a mirror—prism

FIGURE 1.4. The parallax effect

As seen by viewing lens

As photographed by taking lens

FIGURE 1.5
Types of shutters

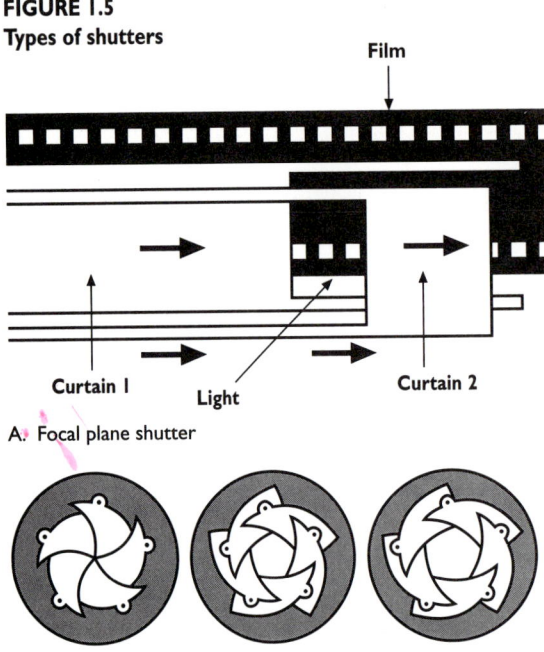

A. Focal plane shutter

B. Leaf shutter

arrangement. When the focusing ring is turned to focus the lens, the prism also turns, bringing the reflected image together with the direct image when the camera is in focus.

In the **ground-glass system,** light from the lens is projected onto a viewing screen. Thus, when the focusing ring is turned to focus the lens, the photographer sees the same image the lens "sees" and can judge when the camera is in focus. Various screens that are available to make focusing more precise are discussed in Chapter 2.

• A **shutter** controls exposure of the film to light by opening and closing at various speeds. It thus determines the length of time light enters the camera and strikes the film. Shutters are of two types: the focal plane shutter and the leaf shutter (Figure 1.5).

The **focal plane shutter** is built into the camera body at a point directly in front of the film. (It receives its name from the fact that it resides just forward of the **plane of focus,** or area where the image projected from the lens should be sharpest.) The focal plane shutter usually consists of two overlapping curtains forming an adjustable window. The spring-powered window moves across the film and exposes it as it moves. The **leaf shutter** is located within the lens and consists of several small overlapping spring-powered metal blades. As the blades open, they form a circular opening through which light passes until the end of the exposure, when the blades close again. The time interval between opening and closing is adjustable for both types of shutters. The shutter control mechanism—the shutter speed dial—on the camera is shown in Figure 1.6 and discussed further in Chapter 2.

Both types of shutters have advantages and disadvantages. A camera with a focal plane shutter can use lenses that are less expensive because a shutter mechanism does not have to be built into each one. A focal plane shutter is also generally capable of faster shutter speeds because its design does not require the curtains to reverse direction during the exposure, as is the case with the blades of a leaf shutter. Leaf shutters, on the other hand, are quieter than focal plane shutters, which produce a distinct snap when released. Leaf shutters can also be used with electronic flash at higher speeds. A focal plane shutter is generally

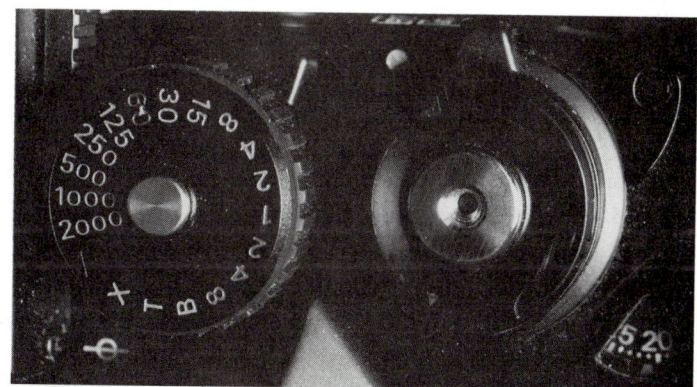

FIGURE 1.6.
Shutter speed dial

FIGURE 1.7.
Aperture ring

limited to maximum speeds of $^1/_{60}$, $^1/_{125}$, or $^1/_{250}$ of a second (in some newer cameras) with flash because the window does not uncover the film completely at any one time at higher speeds. Beginners should remember that the focal plane shutter is fragile and easily damaged and they should not touch it.

• An **aperture** also controls the exposure of film to light, but by establishing the size of the lens opening. The aperture consists of overlapping metal pieces that move to form a circular opening. The size of the opening is controlled by the aperture ring (Figure 1.7). When the ring is turned in one direction, it rotates the metal pieces toward the outside of the circle and increases the size of the aperture. Turning the aperture ring in the other direction moves the metal pieces toward the center and reduces the size of the aperture. Larger aperture sizes allow more light through the lens; smaller sizes allow less. The net result is that the aperture controls the brightness or quantity of light to which the film is exposed. Aperture sizes are measured in f-stops and are discussed in Chapter 2.

• A **lens** projects a reversed image of the subject onto the film. In its simplest form, a lens is a single element, a solid piece of curved glass. Other optical elements of varying shapes are usually added to a lens to enable it to project a sharp image without distortion under all light conditions. The lens, sitting as it does between the subject and the film, sorts out various light rays, focuses them, and directs them to reproduce the subject faithfully on film.

• The **body** of the camera houses all the parts and protects the film from light. Some camera bodies have a permanently attached lens. Others have no lens attached, but are designed to hold interchangeable lenses.

• A **film-holding mechanism** holds the film tightly in place to record the light rays focused on it by the lens, and a **film-advancing mechanism** moves the film from left to right in order to expose as many pictures as are on the strip of film. The type of device for holding the film depends on the type of film used by the camera.

All 35 mm cameras use strips of film 35 mm wide and 2 to 3 feet in length. The film is packaged inside a cassette, which is held inside the camera, nearly always on the left side. The free end of the film attaches to a take-up spool on the right side. A pressure plate holds the film flat against the back of the camera. Some types of cameras use roll film, similar to 35 mm film, but wider. Most roll film is 60 mm wide and comes wrapped around a spool with a paper backing to protect it from light. It is held in the camera much the same way as 35 mm film. Some larger cameras, however, use sheets rather than strips of film. Sheet film must be first loaded into special film holders, which can then be inserted into the back of the camera to take one picture at a time.

Types of Cameras

There are four major types of cameras: view camera, viewfinder, twin-lens reflex, and single-lens reflex. Categorized by the kind of viewing system it has, each has distinct advantages and disadvantages.

• **View cameras** (Figure 1.8) resemble accordions. The lens is in the front, a viewing screen is in the back, and a flexible bellows sits between them. The design dates back to the earliest days of photography. Although simple, the view camera is very flexible and has capabilities possessed by no other type of camera. The lens produces an inverted image on a ground-glass plate at the rear of the camera. The image is composed and focused on the ground glass. To take the picture, a piece of film is inserted in front of the ground glass.

A view camera generally uses sheet film of 4" x 5" or larger. The large negative is capable of great sharpness and detail. But perhaps the greatest advantage of the view camera is the power it gives the photographer in composing the picture, in adjusting the field of focus, and in controlling perspective. The greatest disadvantage of the camera is its bulk. A view camera must be used on a tripod

FIGURE 1.8.
View camera

(Sinar F1; published with permission, Sinar Bron, Inc.)

and is relatively slow to operate. And because the image projected on the viewing screen is dim, photographers using the camera have to put a dark cloth over their heads and the back of the camera, something that has characterized this camera since its appearance in the nineteenth century.

• **Viewfinder cameras** (Figure 1.9) see their subjects through a small hole containing a simple lens that provides an image of how the final picture will look. The light from the subject travels separately through the lens to the film and through the viewfinder to the eye. Thus, the viewfinder and the taking lens see the subject from two levels and parallax error results. What you see in the viewfinder is slightly different from what will be recorded on film. Sophisticated viewfinder cameras compensate for the parallax problem at all but very close distances.

The greatest weakness of the viewfinder camera is that it generally cannot be used with telephoto lenses and is difficult to use with close-up lenses. The biggest advantages of viewfinder cameras are their compact construction, light weight, quietness, and fast handling. They are also easy to focus in low-light areas.

Better viewfinder cameras include a rangefinder focusing mechanism, and thus the term **rangefinder** camera is used almost interchangeably with **viewfinder** camera. The first commercially successful 35 mm camera, the Leica, was a rangefinder design. Rangefinder Leicas, although very expensive, are still used by many professionals.

FIGURE 1.9. Viewfinder camera

(Pentax IQ Zoom 105 Super; published with permission, Pentax Corp.)

FIGURE 1.10.
Twin-lens reflex camera

(Mamiya® C330; published with permission, Mamiya American Corp.)

• **Twin-lens reflex cameras** (Figure 1.10), as their name suggests, have two lenses. One is used for viewing and focusing; the other, for taking the picture itself. The two matched lenses are located, one above the other, on the front of the camera. The picture is composed and focused on a ground-glass viewing screen on the top of the camera. The camera is called a reflex because the light that forms the image on the ground glass is reflected off a mirror to turn the image right-side up. Twin-lens reflexes generally use roll film.

The chief advantages of twin-lens reflex cameras are their simplicity, durability, and quietness. The larger negative tends to give a sharper and more detailed enlargement. Also, because the photographer uses the camera by looking down into it from above, he or she can use it at waist level or even ground level easily. It can also be held directly overhead to gain a high angle of view. The two disadvantages of the camera are its parallax error, which makes close-up work next to impossible, and its inflexibility. Few twin-lens reflexes can accept different types of lenses, a fact that considerably limits their usefulness.

• **Single-lens reflex cameras** (Figure 1.11) allow the photographer to see directly through the lens that takes the picture (Figure 1.12). Light from the lens is reflected by a mirror inside the camera upward into the viewing system.

FIGURE 1.11.
Single-lens reflex
camera

*(Nikon N70 Autofocus
SLR Camera, published
with permission)*

When the picture is taken, the mirror swings up out of the way, allowing light to pass through the camera body and shutter, to the film at the back of the camera. The viewing system contains a prism that inverts the reversed image coming from the lens and projects it onto a ground-glass viewing screen. The photographer thus views the scene as it appears before the camera. Most single-lens reflex cameras take 35 mm film. Some expensive professional models take roll film, which gives larger negatives, usually 2¼" square.

The major advantage of single-lens reflex cameras is the flexibility the viewing system gives. Because the photographer sees exactly what the film will record, there is no parallax error and nearly any type of lens may be attached. The camera is ideal for extreme close-up work and is equally adept when used with long telephoto lenses. Its extreme adaptability has made the 35 mm single-lens reflex by far the most popular of all camera types. But it is not without disadvantages. The addition of the mirror and viewing system tends to make the camera heavier and more bulky than 35 mm viewfinder cameras. And the movement of the mirror makes the camera rather noisy and causes camera shake.

Choice of a Camera

The selection of a camera depends entirely on the way you intend to use it. But it is probably safe to say that the serious student of photography should begin with a 35 mm single-lens reflex unless overriding considerations dictate some other type. The camera's flexibility allows you to explore many avenues of photography and to do so relatively inexpensively because 35 mm film allows many pictures per roll. As your skills develop and your photographic interests become more specialized, you may wish to obtain a different type of camera. But until then, the single-lens reflex offers you unparalleled opportunities to experiment and learn.

But even after narrowing your choice to a 35 mm single-lens reflex, you still have a wide variety of camera makes and models to choose from. They are available with such an overwhelming assortment of features that you almost expect one of the major camera manufacturers to introduce a model one day that will wash and dry the dishes when you're not busy photographing.

In the meantime, you still have to select between models with automatic versus manual exposure, with interchangeable versus fixed lenses, with greater or lesser flexibility in the attachments they will accept, and so on. Let's look at some of the major features available.

- **Built-in light meters.** Nearly all single-lens reflex cameras today have a built-in light meter located behind the reflex mirror, where the meter monitors the light coming through the lens. Depending on the model of the camera you have, you may interact with the meter in any one of three possible exposure modes: manual exposure, automatic exposure, or programmed exposure.

Some cameras with built-in light meters have **manual exposure**—that is, you manipulate both the aperture and the shutter speed to set the exposure indicated by the meter. Other cameras have **automatic exposure,** where you set either the shutter speed or aperture and the camera selects the other setting

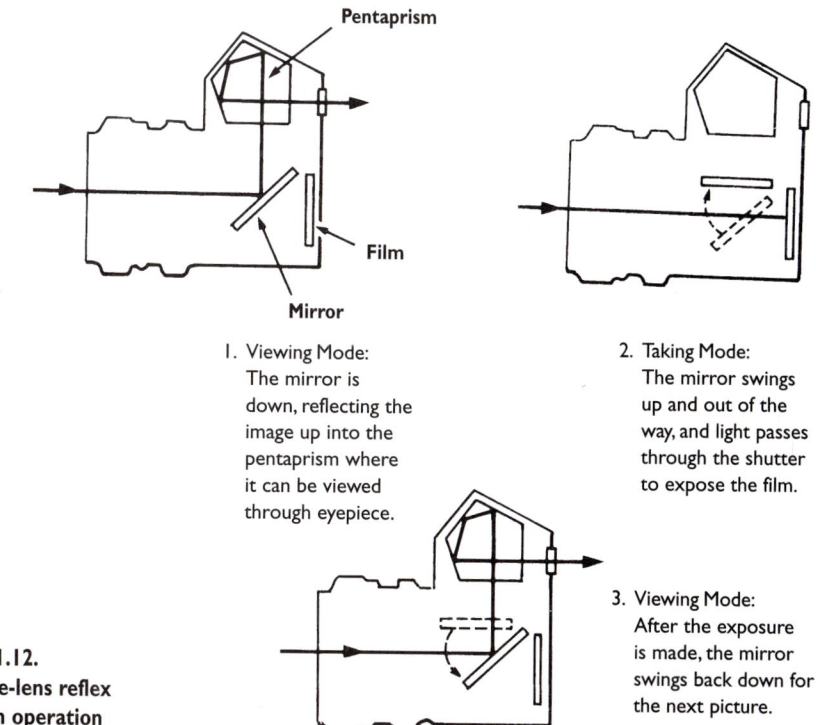

Pentaprism

Film

Mirror

1. Viewing Mode: The mirror is down, reflecting the image up into the pentaprism where it can be viewed through eyepiece.

2. Taking Mode: The mirror swings up and out of the way, and light passes through the shutter to expose the film.

3. Viewing Mode: After the exposure is made, the mirror swings back down for the next picture.

FIGURE 1.12.
The single-lens reflex camera in operation

FIGURE 1.13.
A camera panel display showing shutter speed, aperture, exposures taken (19), exposure mode (manual), and light reading

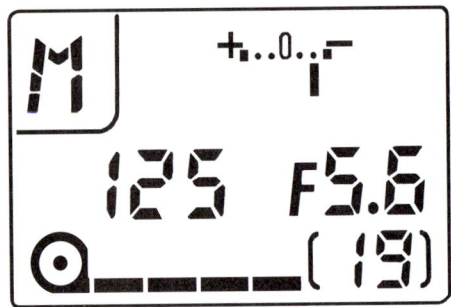

to produce correct exposure. Still other cameras have a **programmed exposure mode**, where the camera makes all exposure settings with no intervention from you. Many modern cameras combine two or more of these metering modes and allow you to choose between them. Most of these cameras are heavily electronic and use a panel display (Figure 1.13) to indicate the metering mode as well as other important camera information.

Since all three exposure modes are capable of accurate exposures, the choice is largely a matter of personal preference. Some photographers find automatic exposure or programmed exposure a convenience and say it lets them concentrate more on the picture itself. Others say setting the exposure manually is hardly difficult and want the extra sense of control over the exposure.

You should not get a camera with a built-in light meter that does not allow you to override the automatic or programmed feature. This limitation can be severe in certain lighting situations. Fortunately, it is a limitation found on few cameras. If you choose a camera without a built-in light meter, hand-held light meters (Figure 1.14) are available to do the job of monitoring light.

• **Interchangeable lenses.** If you plan to further develop your interest in photography, you should buy a camera that will take interchangeable lenses.

Eventually you are certain to feel limited by a choice of but one lens. The ability to use wide angle, telephoto, or macro (close-up) lenses greatly extends the versatility of your camera.

• **Assorted power features.** Now, what about all those features: shutter speed ranges, interchangeable viewfinders, electronic meter readouts, ability to take motor drives or winders, and so forth? Your pocketbook will probably have a great deal to say about these decisions. It does, however, make some sense to buy a little more camera than you need at the moment. That way, it can meet your needs as your abilities develop.

• **How the camera feels.** In choosing a camera, there is one consideration that is more important than simply accumulating bells and whistles: How does the camera feel? Are you comfortable with it? When faced by camera brochures with multicolored charts extolling all the features of this or that model, how the camera feels may seem a rather trivial consideration. If it makes you feel any better, design engineers have a sophisticated word for it—ergonomics.

The feel of the camera is an important consideration if you and your camera are to become one functional unit. To photograph comfortably, your camera must feel as though it is a part of you. Does it fit your hand? Is the viewfinder easy to look through? (That is especially important if you wear glasses.) Are the camera controls easily accessible without taking your eye from the viewfinder? Is the camera the right weight? Will the camera be easy to carry with you?

Before you buy a camera, try it out under your normal shooting conditions. If you plan to use it in low-light conditions, try it there. Its viewfinder may be too dim to allow easy focusing. If you plan to take candid pictures of people, try that. It may be too noisy to allow you to work unobtrusively. Talk to other people who own that camera. Find out what problems they might have had and what they like about it. Talk to your instructor or advanced photographers about the suitability of the camera for your needs.

FIGURE 1.14. Hand-held light meters

A. Incident light meter with built-in microcomputer (Sekonic Digi Master Model L-718; published with permission, Sekonic-R.T.S.]

B. Reflected light type exposure meter (Sekonic Auto-Leader Model L-188; published with permission, Sekonic-R.T.S.)

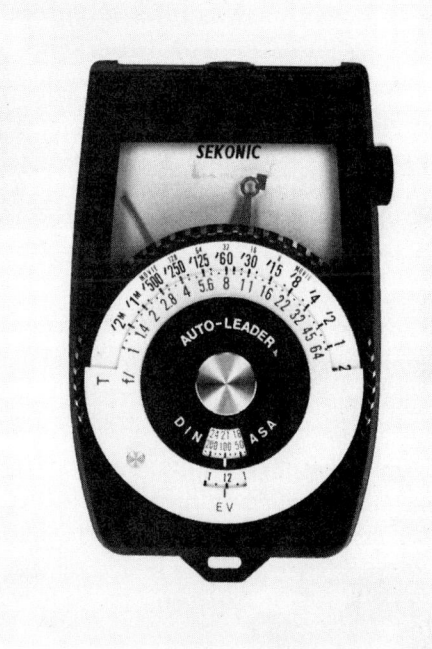

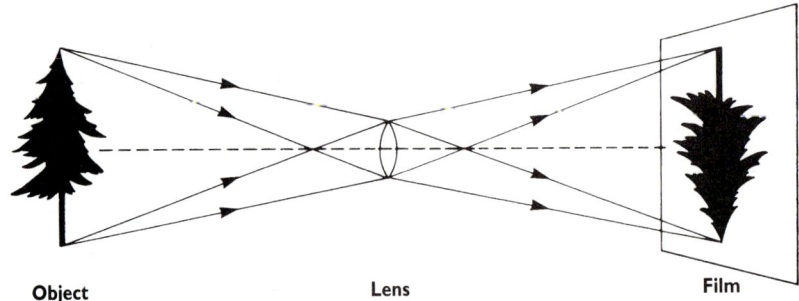

FIGURE 1.15. Diagram of a lens transmitting reflected light

● **Used cameras.** Sometimes you can find a bargain on a used camera. But first make sure it is in good working order. Check especially to make sure all shutter speeds are working properly, that the meter gives accurate readings, that the back closes securely, that film advances smoothly, that the lens mount isn't worn, that both the aperture and focusing rings operate smoothly, and that the lens itself is free of nicks and scratches. Shoot a test roll and process it to check overall operation. If you still aren't sure, have someone who knows cameras check it over for you.

Types of Lenses

Lenses gather the rays of light coming from the scene to be photographed and project them as reversed images onto the film at the back of the camera (Figure 1.15). It sounds rather simple, yet lenses are probably the most powerful part of a camera system. To many photographers, a camera body is just something to which you attach your lenses. Lenses are what give you creative control over the look of your photograph.

Many cameras use interchangeable lenses. The difference in lenses comes from their **focal length**—that is, the distance between the optical center of the lens and the point where it focuses (plane of focus). Focal length determines the size of the image formed by the lens, called **magnification,** and how much of the scene is included in the image, called the **angle of view.** In practice, focal length also controls the perspective of the image—that is, the relationship between the sizes of foreground and background subjects.

Photographers also speak of the "speed" of a lens. It is a measure of how much light it transmits to the film. A fast lens has a larger maximum aperture and lets through more light. A slower lens has a smaller aperture and lets through less light. Faster lenses are larger in diameter and generally more expensive than slower lenses of the same focal length.

Depending on their focal lengths, lenses are generally classified as normal, telephoto, or wide angle (Figure 1.16). In addition, there are special-purpose lenses whose use is dictated by features other than focal length.

• **Normal lenses** have a focal length that is the same as (or very close to) the diagonal measurement of the film size with which they are used. For 35 mm film, the normal focal length is 50 mm. For 2¼" x 2¼" film, it is between 75 and 85 mm. For 4" x 5" film, it is 135 to 165 mm. The normal lens is the center point in the spectrum of focal lengths. It "sees" the subject in roughly the same way a person does when looking straight ahead (Figure 1.17B). A normal lens is the one most often purchased with a camera, and it is a useful general-purpose lens.

• **Wide angle lenses** have focal lengths shorter than a normal lens. Common sizes in 35 mm photography include the 35 mm, 28 mm, 24 mm, and 20 mm. Lenses shorter than 20 mm are commonly called "fish-eyes" because they produce a distorted circular image. Wide angles, as the name suggests, capture a wider angle of view than a normal lens (Figure 1.17A). They have less magnification

FIGURE 1.16. Four types of lenses: wide angle, normal, telephoto, zoom

FIGURE 1.17.
Photographs taken from the same vantage point with different lenses

A. Taken with wide angle lens (20 mm)

B. Taken with normal lens (55 mm)

than a normal lens and tend to push background further away from foreground. As a result, they appear to add depth to the image.

Wide angle lenses are useful for scenics where a panoramic view is desired. They are also frequently used in tight quarters where no other lens offers a sufficient angle of view. Because they distort the image, the shorter "fish eyes" are sometimes used to create interesting graphic effects in the photograph. Many photographers prefer wide angles for candids of people because they force the photographer to work close to the subject, producing a look of immediacy and intimacy that often adds power to the picture.

- **Telephoto lenses** have focal lengths longer than the normal lens. Common telephoto focal lengths in 35 mm photography include 85 mm, 105 mm, 135 mm, 200 mm, 300 mm, 400 mm, 500 mm, 600 mm, 1,000 mm, and 1,200 mm. The telephoto gives a narrow angle of view and magnifies the subject by bringing it closer to the camera (Figures 1.17C and D). The longer the focal length, the narrower the view and the greater the magnification. Telephotos also exhibit a perspective effect often referred to as "telephoto compression." A telephoto tends

FIGURE 1.17.
(continued)

C. Taken with telephoto lens (105 mm)

D. Taken with telephoto lens (180 mm)

to reduce differences in size between foreground and background objects, thus forcing foreground and background into one plane, as though they were compressed.

Telephoto lenses are most frequently used when it is impossible to get close to the subject. Common applications include wildlife photography, sports photography, theater photography, or candid shots of people where the photographer wishes to remain unnoticed. They are also commonly used in portraiture, where they maintain a pleasing perspective. The 105 mm, for instance, is often used for head-and-shoulders portraits.

Perspective can be controlled by using different lenses. Perspective is the relative size of foreground versus background objects. If you were to shoot the same picture using a variety of focal length lenses and move the camera each time to keep the foreground subject the same size, you would find that background objects would change size in the photograph (Figure 1.18). Wide angle lenses emphasize the foreground and the distance between foreground and background. Telephoto lenses emphasize the background and compress the distance between foreground and background.

FIGURE 1.18. Using different lenses to control perspective

A. Taken with wide angle lens (20 mm)

B. Taken with normal lens (55 mm); camera moved back to keep foreground and subject the same size

C. Taken with telephoto lens (105 mm); camera moved further back

D. Taken with telephoto lens (180 mm); camera moved still further back

- **Zoom lenses** do not have a fixed focal length. The focal length of the lens can instead be adjusted over a range of focal lengths. A commonly found model allows adjustment from 35 mm to 135 mm. In effect, the photographer owns a 35 mm lens, a 135 mm lens, and all lenses between. Many zoom lenses offer a macro mode, which allows close-up photography. While zoom lenses offer a great deal of flexibility in a single package, they are not the answer to everyone's need for lenses. Zoom lenses tend to be bulkier than fixed focal length lenses. They are not quite as sharp unless a very high quality model is used. And they are usually slower than an equivalent fixed lens.

- **Autofocus lenses** can be electronically focused by circuitry built into the camera body. In use, you superimpose a tiny viewfinder autofocus spot over the subject, press a button on the camera, and the lens automatically rotates to the sharpest point of focus. Like most things automatic, autofocus lenses do have limitations. If your subject is standing behind something that the autofocus feature can confuse for the subject, for instance, it may focus on the wrong object. In addition, the autofocusing mechanism may not operate well with low-contrast subjects or strongly backlit subjects. However, most autofocus cameras allow you to switch to manual focus mode, so these are usually simple problems to correct.

- **Special-purpose lenses** are also available. Macro lenses, for example, are designed for close-up work. A true macro lens allows you to focus close enough to make a negative image that is the same size as the subject itself. Thus, you can take a picture of a paper clip and the negative image will be as large as the paper clip itself. Most macro lenses are 50 mm or 100 mm focal lengths and can be used as any lens of the same focal length. They are not as fast as a non-macro lens of equivalent focal length, however.

Other special-purpose lenses have built-in flash units for technical and scientific use. Some can shift up and down, or from side to side, to allow more control in architectural photography. Some have special optical corrections for use in copying flat subjects like paintings or printed pages.

Choice of a Lens

Buying lenses is like buying cameras: Your choice depends on your needs and the amount of money you have to spend. As with cameras, it is a good idea to start simply and add lenses as your needs require them.

Talk to fellow students, your instructor, and advanced photographers for advice on what lens or lenses to buy initially. Again, although most people begin with a normal lens, it is often not the ideal choice. This statement is particularly true if your budget allows buying more than one lens and you can afford to get both a telephoto and a wide angle to begin with.

Frequently, the speed of the lens (its maximum aperture) is as important a consideration as its focal length. Many focal lengths are available in two or more maximum apertures. If you often shoot in low-light levels, or need a brighter viewfinder to make focusing easier, then a faster lens is probably your best choice.

REVIEW
Questions

1. What are the seven basic parts of a typical 35 mm camera?

2. How does each part work?

3. What is a view camera?

4. What is a viewfinder camera?

5. What is a twin-lens reflex camera?

6. What is a single-lens reflex camera?

7. What factors are important in choosing what camera to buy?

8. What are the main types of camera lenses?

9. How does each lens affect the photo taken by the camera?

10. What are the most important considerations in choosing a lens?

CHAPTER TWO

OPERATING
The Camera

"Self-Portrait with Newsboy" by Lewis Hine, 1908

TWO

OPERATING
the Camera

"Self-Portrait with Newsboy" by Lewis Hine, 1908
(Courtesy of the Library of Congress)

Lewis Hine's photographs of the exploitation of child labor engage the viewer in large part because of the unblinking look of its subjects—always gazing into the camera. His photos are also compelling because of the unusual juxtaposition of child against the backdrop of work (dark spaces containing huge machines about to gobble up the tiny creatures in their midst). Although he traveled around with fifty pounds of heavy equipment (a stand camera, tripod, and flash tray), Hine often had to work fast lest he be discovered by the disreputable men enslaving the children. He often presented himself as something other than a photographer and made notes surreptitiously. In this photo of a newsboy, the shadow of Hine and his camera seems to undercut the objectivity that characterizes most of his work. It may also represent an admission that Hine's objectivity was very personal and passionate.

WITH EXPERIENCE, the process of operating a camera becomes almost automatic, like driving a car or riding a bicycle. At first, however, you have to learn how to use your camera—and in a way that is easiest for you.

Part of the process is selecting the film and loading it into the camera properly. Operating a camera also requires that you master the seemingly complex steps of adjusting the exposure, setting the shutter speed, and focusing the camera.

Selecting 35 mm Film

Most types of 35 mm film are available in rolls of 24 or 36 exposures. The 36-exposure rolls are more economical per frame. But you may want to begin by using 24-exposure rolls until you master film processing, because shorter rolls are somewhat easier to handle in the darkroom. The important issue, however, in selecting a film is its speed.

Film speed

Film is differentiated by its **speed**—that is, its sensitivity to light. Film speeds are noted by their **ISO Index**, a number designation assigned by the International Standards Organization.

The ISO number recently replaced the ASA (American Standards Association) number as the standard for identifying film speed. But only the name changed; the rating system and numbers are the same. Thus, even though your camera and light meter are marked for ASA numbers, they will work just as well with the new ISO index. Films, cameras, and light meters may also be marked with another sensitivity scale called the DIN rating. DIN stands for *Deutsche Industrie Norm* (German Industry Standard) and is widely used in Europe.

In the ISO rating system, high numbers mean films that are very sensitive to light. In the jargon of photography, they are called **fast** films because you can

FIGURE 2.1. Medium, fast, and super-fast films

often use a faster shutter speed than with a **slower** film—that is, one that has a lower rating and is less sensitive to light.

Film sensitivity, or speed, combines with lighting conditions to determine the camera aperture and shutter speed settings needed for a properly exposed negative. A film with an ISO index twice that of another film is exactly twice as sensitive to light—that is, it will require half as much light to expose it properly. For example, a film with an ISO of 400 requires half as much exposure as an ISO 200 film. Therefore, you need to use an aperture one stop smaller or a shutter speed one notch faster than with an ISO 200 film. On the other hand, a film with an ISO index of 100 requires twice as much light (one stop greater) as an ISO 200 film.

Film ratings are divided into several categories:

Slow speed (ISO 25 to ISO 50),
Medium speed (ISO 100 to ISO 200),
Fast speed (ISO 400 to ISO 500),
Super-fast (ISO 1,000 and above).

In general, faster films are needed when shooting in low-level light and slower films can be used only when light levels are relatively high. Commonly used fast and slow films are shown in Figure 2.1.

If you are just getting started in photography, it is a good idea to begin with one of the "fast" black and white films. These films allow you to shoot both indoors and outdoors under most light conditions. And, as a bonus, they tend to be more forgiving of exposure errors than slower speed films. After you've

FIGURE 2.2.
Manufacturer's
instructions for
Kodak T-Max 400 Film
printed inside the box

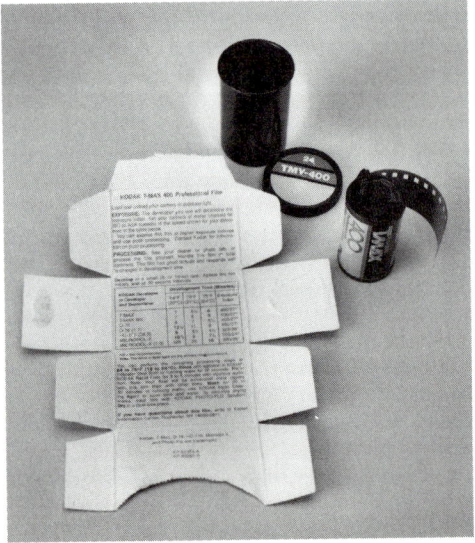

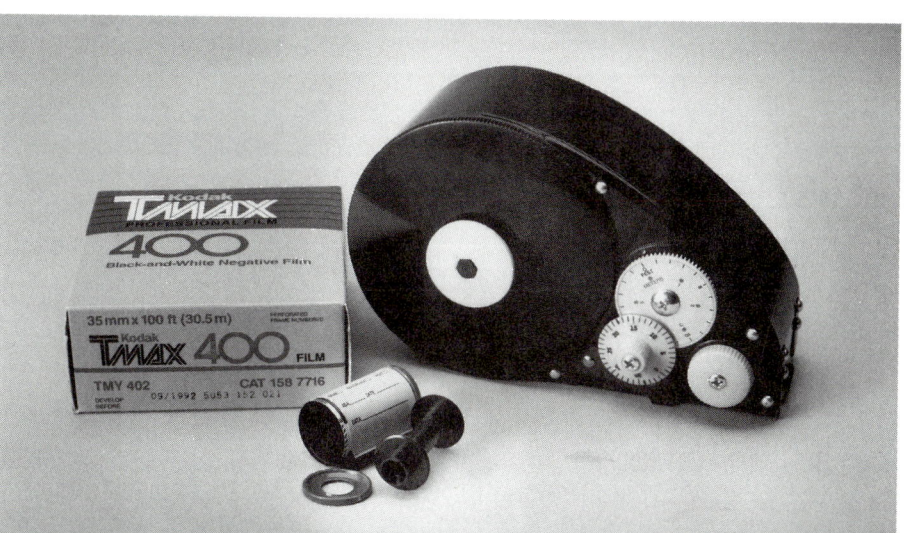

FIGURE 2.3. Bulk loading equipment: A 100-foot roll of film, bulk loader, and reusable cassette

mastered the use of any of these films, then you'll be ready to tackle the somewhat more challenging slower films.

Whatever film speed you choose, you'll need to set your meter accordingly after you load the film. Most cameras have an ISO (or ASA) dial which can be turned to the correct film speed. Some newer cameras set the film speed automatically for **DX coded film.** DX coded film cassettes are imprinted with a pattern of black and silver squares which represent the film's ISO index. A series of small electrical contacts inside the camera body translates this pattern into the approximate film speed for the meter. Automatic DX coding can save you from the error of forgetting to set the ISO index when you change films. However, if you can't override the DX coding, it will make it difficult to push process film and to use bulk loaded film. Push processing and bulk loading will be discussed later, but suffice it to say that you should think twice before buying a camera that does not allow you to set the film speed manually when needed.

You should read and save the manufacturer's instructions packaged with the film (Figure 2.2). These instructions include information on exposure settings for all types of lighting and often give suggestions about developing the film.

Bulk Loading Film

You can usually cut your film costs nearly in half by buying film in bulk rolls and loading it into cassettes yourself. Most common 35 mm films are available in 100-foot rolls, which yield the equivalent of 20 36-exposure rolls once loaded into cassettes. You use a bulk loader (Figure 2.3) to transfer the film from the long roll to shorter lengths inside reusable film cassettes that will fit your camera. The bulk loader has a large chamber to accommodate the bulk roll and a smaller chamber to hold the cassette. Once the bulk roll is inside the bulk loader, the job of transferring the film to the cassettes can be done in room light. Bulk loading is a relatively simple process that will probably be well worth your while if you shoot much film.

Loading a 35 mm Camera

When loading film into the camera, it is important to stand in subdued light or to turn your back to the sun so that the camera is shaded. You begin by checking to see that the camera has no film in it. If you can turn the rewind knob in the direction of the arrow marked on it with no resistance, the camera is empty. When you open the back of the camera, you should always be careful not to touch the pressure plate or the shutter curtain.

In most cameras, you insert the film cassette in a cassette chamber on the left wide of the camera and draw the film across the back of the camera to the take-up reel. You put slight tension on the film with the film-advance lever and make sure you engage the sprocket wheel in the film sprocket holes along the edge of the film. After closing the camera, the last step is to turn the rewind knob gently in the direction of the arrow to take the slack out of the film.

You will need to shoot off two or three waste exposures to move exposed film out of the way and position unexposed film behind the shutter. At the same time, you can watch the rewind knob to make sure it turns backwards. If it does, the film is advancing properly. If it doesn't, you should open the camera to see what went wrong.

Adjusting the Exposure

Correct exposure involves getting the right amount of light to the film. Too much light will **overexpose** the film. Too little light will **underexpose** the film. Neither will result in a satisfactory negative, and without a good negative, you won't be able to make a good print. The camera exposure is set with two controls: the aperture ring and the shutter speed dial. Exposure is determined by using a light meter. In some cameras, meters are built in. With others, you must use a separate (hand-held) meter. In either case, the film speed rating—the ISO index—must be set properly on the meter or the entire roll will be incorrectly exposed.

Aperture: controlling light intensity

The aperture controls the intensity of the light passing through the lens. As can be seen in Figure 2.4, a large aperture lets through a lot of light, while a small aperture allows little light to pass through. The size of the aperture, also called the lens opening, is designated by the f-stop.

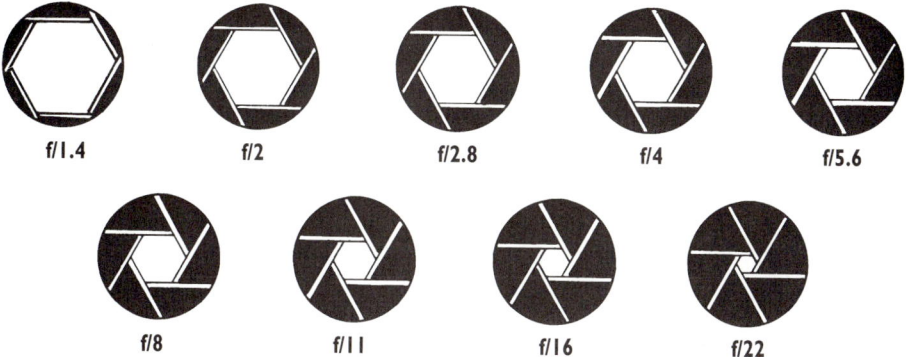

f/1.4   f/2   f/2.8   f/4   f/5.6

f/8   f/11   f/16   f/22

FIGURE 2.4. Diagram of apertures showing comparative size of openings at various f-stops

F-stops on the camera are noted—usually on the lens barrel—in a rather odd series of numbers like this:

1.4, 2, 2.8, 4, 5.6, 8, 11, 16, 22.

Such numbers are a shorthand way of expressing fractions. They give the ratio of the focal length of the lens (50 mm or 55 mm for a normal lens) to the physical diameter of the aperture opening. The ratios are used so that an f-stop on one lens gives the same exposure as the same f-stop on another lens. Thus, f/2 on a telephoto lens admits as much light as f/2 on a wide angle lens.

The larger f-stop numbers (like f/16) indicate smaller lens openings; the smaller numbers (like f/4) represent larger openings. When you change the lens opening from one f-stop to the next, you are adjusting the aperture "one stop." The f-stop series has been arranged so that each such change either doubles the intensity of light or cuts it in half. When you go down to the next smaller aperture (from f/4 to f/5.6, for instance), you are "stopping down" one stop and letting in half as much light. When you move a stop up to a larger aperture (say from f/8 to f/5.6), you are "opening up" the lens and allowing twice as much light in.

Shutter speed: Controlling exposure length

The shutter speed controls the length of the exposure. A closed shutter means that no light may enter the camera body and strike the film. Opening the shutter allows light to strike the film until the shutter closes again. Shutter speed, then, is the length of time the shutter remains open. Simple cameras often have a single, fixed shutter speed. Adjustable cameras have a wide range of shutter speeds.

Shutter speeds appear on a camera in a series like this:

B, 1, 2, 4, 8, 15, 30, 60, 125, 250, 500.

These numbers are a quick way of noting fractions of a second. A shutter speed of 30 means 1/30 of a second, for instance. The larger numbers thus represent smaller fractions, or shorter exposure times.

Camera shutter settings are organized so that each one is either half or double the length of time of the one next to it. For example, moving from a setting of 30 to one of 60 lets in half as much light because the shutter stays open only half as long. Going from 500 to 250, on the other hand, allows in twice as much light because the shutter is open twice as long. Most cameras include shutter speeds larger than $1/$ second. Speeds like 4s or 2s denote speeds of 4 seconds and 2 seconds. In addition, most cameras include a "B" shutter speed, which allows you to hold the shutter open for as long as you want. When the shutter is set to "B", the shutter opens when you depress the shutter release button and stays open for as long as you hold it down. The "B" stands for "Bulb" and is sometimes used for special effects in flash photography.

As you have probably noticed, the shutter speed series and aperture series parallel one another. In both, each time you move a notch up or down the scale, you halve or double the amount of light reaching the film during exposure. This is no coincidence, of course. The exposure controls were designed so that you can trade off shutter speeds and apertures.

The law of reciprocity

The basic principle of exposure is called the **law of reciprocity.** It simply means that you can reciprocate (or compensate for) a change in one exposure control with a change in the other. That is, you can trade off shutter speeds for apertures and vice versa.

You can trade off a shutter speed for an aperture setting because both shutter speed and aperture affect things besides exposure. Various settings will give the same exposure, but not the same picture. For instance, there will be differences in the ability of the camera to record moving subjects without blur. The way a camera records action is controlled by the shutter speed. And there will be differences in the overall sharpness of the picture from foreground to background. This overall sharpness of the image is called "depth of field" by photographers, and it is controlled by the aperture.

Here is how the law of reciprocity works. Say your meter says you will obtain a correct exposure using a shutter speed of 1/60 of a second and an aperture of f/8. If you change your shutter speed from 1/60 to 1/125, you will allow half as much light to reach the film because the exposure time will be cut in half. But you can compensate for the decrease by doubling the intensity of the light striking the film—that is, by opening the aperture from f/8 to f/5.6. Thus, 1/125 at f/5.6 will give the same exposure as 1/60 at f/8.

You can continue making alterations: Speed the shutter up to 1/250 and compensate by doubling the light intensity again by changing the aperture to f/4. Or, you can go in the other direction from the original settings of 1/60 at f/8. Slowing the shutter down to 1/30 will let in twice as much light. But you can compensate for the increase by changing the aperture from f/8 to f/11 to decrease

TABLE 2.1 Equivalent exposure settings

Appearance of moving subjects	Shutter speed	Aperture setting	Overall sharpness (depth of field)
blurred, fuzzy	1/8	f /22	large
	1/15	f/16	
	1/30	f/11	
	1/60	f/8	
	1/125	f /5.6	
	1/250	f/4	
	1/500	f /2.8	
	1/1000	f/2	
sharp, clear	1/2000	f 1.4	shallow

TWO

the light intensity. By continuing the trade-off process, you can create an entire series of equivalent exposure settings, as shown in Table 2.1.

If you are using a hand-held light meter, the series of equivalent exposure settings is usually obvious because the meter's dial gives them all to you at once. A built-in meter, on the other hand, gives them to you one at a time. But even the built-in meter will yield the same series if you change the shutter speed and aperture settings. If you have a built-in meter, you can try this experiment: Point your camera at something and make a meter reading. Note the shutter speed and aperture settings. Now change the shutter speed to the next fastest speed. Then change the aperture to compensate. You should find that you had to move to the next larger aperture opening. By continuing the process, you will find an exposure setting series similar to the one in the example above. That series will give you the various shutter speed and aperture combinations for the subject you were metering and the speed of the film you were using.

Photographers have devised a shorthand—called the **exposure value**—that can be used to refer to the group of all the shutter speed-aperture combinations that give correct exposure with a certain brightness level. For instance, an aperture of f/2.8 and a shutter speed of 1/60 is equivalent to EV 9. All equivalent shutter speed-aperture combinations—from f/1.4 at 1/250 to f/22 at 1 second—are also EV 9. An exposure value of 10 refers to the set of shutter speed-aperture combinations that would be used when the brightness level is one stop greater—that is, combinations like f/2.8 at 1/125, or f/1.4 at 1/500, or f/22 at 1/2.

Figure 2.5 shows the common range of exposure values in chart form. The diagonal lines intersect all the aperture and shutter speed settings for a particular exposure value. For example, the diagonal line for EV 12 intersects the upper right corner, which represents an aperture of f/1.4 and a shutter speed of 1/2000. If you track that same diagonal line leftward and downward, it next intersects a

FIGURE 2.5.
Chart of
exposure
values

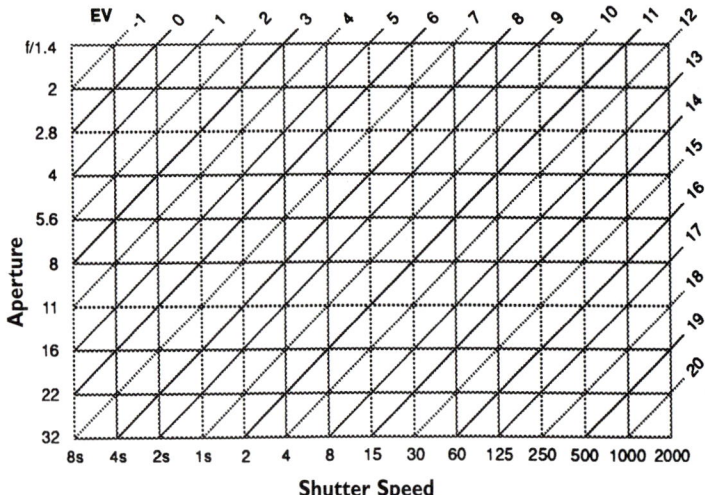

point that represents an aperture of f/2 and a shutter speed of 1/1000 (which the law of reciprocity tells us is equivalent to the first combination). As you continue tracking the diagonal line downward and leftward, you'll find more equivalent combinations of shutter speed and aperture until you finally reach f/32 at 1/4 second.

Although you won't often find exposure values inscribed on modern photographic equipment, you will find charts similar to Figure 2.5 used to depict the exposure characteristics of programmed exposure mode systems. We'll see more about that when we look at exposure meters later in this chapter.

Recording Motion

The shutter speed affects the way cameras record action. If you use a very slow shutter speed to record a moving subject, there is time during the exposure for the subject to trace its image on the film. In other words, you create a blur (Figure 2.6A). A faster shutter speed, on the other hand, tends to "freeze" a moving subject, recording it sharply (Figure 2.6B). By selecting the shutter speed, you can control how much or how little blur a moving subject creates. Other factors affect how moving subjects are recorded: how fast they are moving, how close they are to the camera, and whether they are moving toward the camera or across the viewfinder.

The shutter speed determines how camera movement affects the final image. If the camera is moved during a long exposure, the entire scene in front of the camera will streak across its field of view and produce a blur. Faster shutter speeds decrease the effects of camera movement. A common rule of thumb says that if you hand-hold the camera and want sharp results, you should not use a shutter speed any slower than the focal length of the lens you are using. For a

FIGURE 2.6.
Effects of
shutter speed

A. The camera is held steady and a slow shutter speed allows the moving subject to blur; the background stays sharp.

B. A fast shutter speed freezes the action of both the subject and the background.

C. Moving the camera with the subject, called panning, stops subject motion and blurs the background, creating the impression of movement.

FIGURE 2.7. Focusing aids

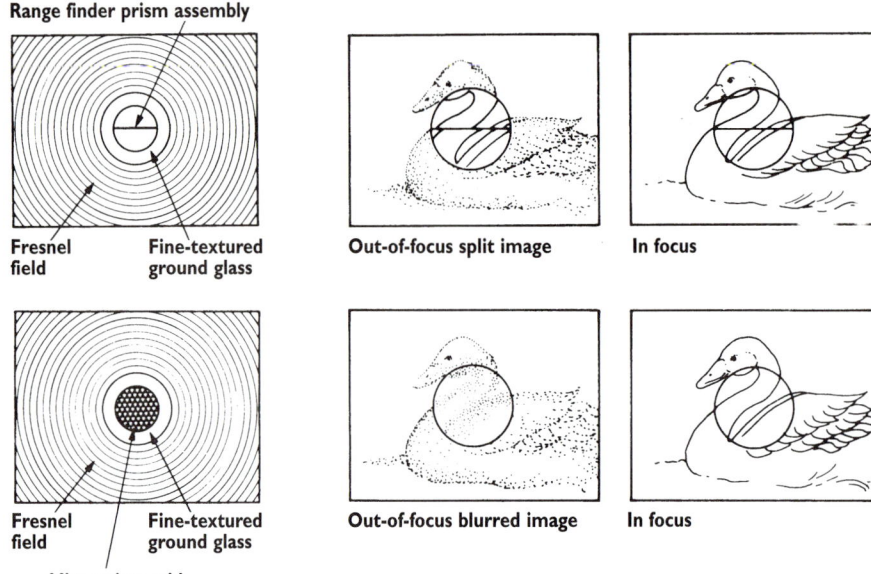

Range finder prism assembly

Fresnel field Fine-textured ground glass

Out-of-focus split image

In focus

Fresnel field Fine-textured ground glass

Microprism grid

Out-of-focus blurred image

In focus

normal (50 mm) lens, then, you should stick to shutter speeds of 1/60 (or 1/50) or faster. For a moderate **telephoto** (say, 135 mm), the minimum speed would be 1/125.

The shutter speed can create special effects. Faster shutter speeds arrest motion and prevent blur, but blur is not always a bad thing. It depends on the picture you want. Many times, blur is an excellent way to produce an image of motion. You can control the degree of blur by controlling the shutter speed (probably 1/30 or slower).

You can also use a technique called **panning,** which involves moving the camera with the subject so the subject maintains the same position in the viewfinder during a long exposure. Because the subject doesn't move relative to the film frame, it is not blurred, but the background is (Figure 2.6C). The result is often an excellent impression of movement from the perspective of the moving subject. Panning takes some practice to do well: You begin the pan before you release the shutter, and continue panning after it has closed. As in any other sport, follow-through is the key to success.

Achieving Sharpness

The camera is in focus when the subject is sharp in the viewfinder. To help you determine focus critically, the ground-glass viewing screens on most 35 mm cameras incorporate various focusing aids (Figure 2.7). **A fresnel lens,**

with concentric line patterns, is used to brighten the outer edges of the screen. The central focusing spot may be either a **split-image rangefinder prism assembly** or a **microprism grid,** or some combination of the two.

The rangefinder focusing spot consists of two small prisms that cause an out-of-focus image to appear split in half in the viewfinder. Focusing brings the two halves of the split image together to form a whole image. Some types of rangefinders are designed to project two superimposed images, rather than a single split image. The superimposed images appear slightly offset from each other when out of focus and are perfectly aligned when in focus. The microprism grid focusing spot consists of many tiny prisms that break up, or exaggerate the blur of, an out-of-focus image. When focused, the image is clear and intact.

A camera can only focus sharply at one distance at a time. If your camera is focused on a subject 6 feet away, only objects 6 feet from the camera will be recorded truly sharp. Other objects, in front of or behind the subject, will be less than sharp. The further the objects are from the plane of focus, the less truly sharp they will be. Some may be so unsharp as to be unidentifiable blurs. Others, those close to the plane of focus, may be so nearly sharp as to be in focus for all practical considerations. They are said to lie within the camera's depth of field.

FIGURE 2.8 Changes in the depth of field at different aperture settings

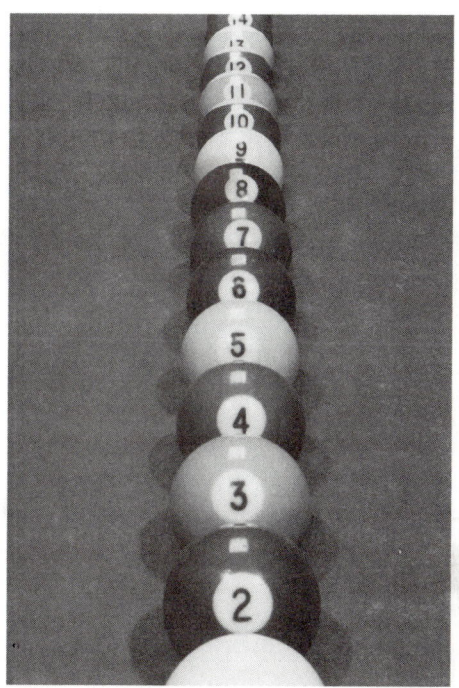

A. f/32   B. f/4

FIGURE 2.9.
Relationship of various aperture settings and depth of field

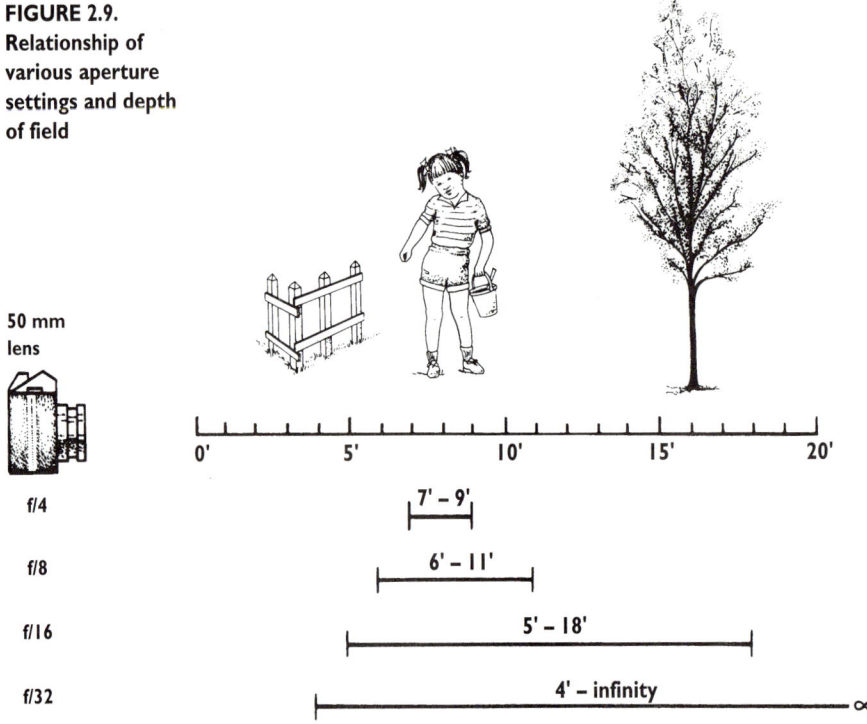

The aperture affects the depth of field. Depth of field means "zone of apparent image sharpness"—that is, the area in front of and behind the point of focus where, although objects won't be exactly sharp, they will be so nearly sharp you won't know the difference. Small apertures (like f/22 or f/32) give a large depth of field, while large apertures (like f/2 or f/4) give a shallow depth of field. Figure 2.8 shows the differences in depth of field in photos taken from the same vantage point with the camera focused in the same spot (the eight ball), but with different aperture settings.

In practice, you can control the zone of apparent sharpness by changing the aperture (Figure 2.9). For example, you may be focused on a subject 8 feet away. With a small aperture like f/32, anything from 4 feet in front of the subject to infinity behind the subject will also be acceptably sharp. By opening the aperture, say, to f/16, you can reduce the depth of field. Now, still focused at 8 feet, only objects from 5 feet away (3 feet in front of the subject) to 18 feet away (10 feet behind the subject) will be sharp. If you open to f/4, the zone of sharpness is reduced to an area from 7 feet away (1 foot in front of the subject) to 9 feet away (1 foot behind the subject).

The distance from camera to subject affects depth of field. If you keep the aperture the same and focus on a subject closer to the camera, the depth of field becomes shallower. On the other hand, if you focus on a subject farther away from the camera, the depth of field is increased. This point is made primarily for the sake of completeness. How far you are from the subject is usually dictated by your picture's composition, or the frame you want to put around the subject. Rarely would you move forward or backward merely to establish a certain depth of field.

The focal length of the lens affects depth of field. If you have a variety of lenses to shoot with, you will notice that they have different depths of field for given aperture settings. Wide angle lenses have a relatively large depth of field. Telephoto lenses have a correspondingly shallow depth of field. Occasionally, the depth of field you wish to establish will determine your choice of lens.

There are two ways of determining the amount of depth of field. Nearly all lenses are inscribed with a depth of field scale. They will tell you, for the aperture you are using, how far forward of and behind the subject will be sharp. The scale gives you distance, but you will have to imagine how the finished picture will look. As an aid to overcoming this problem, many single-lens reflex cameras also have a depth of field preview button. If you use that, you can get a close approximation of the finished image by simply looking through the viewfinder. The button works by actually stopping the lens down to the aperture you have selected. Because the viewfinder goes dim when the lens is stopped down, using the preview feature takes some getting used to.

Depth of field is one of the creative controls of an adjustable camera. There will be times when you want considerable depth of field. If you want to establish a visual relationship between something in the foreground and something in the background, you will need enough depth of field so they are both sharp. There will be other times when you want to limit depth of field. If you are taking a portrait and the subject is standing in front of a busy, distracting background, you will want a shallow depth of field to throw the background out of focus. That way attention will be centered on the subject.

Unloading the Film

When you have completed a roll of film, the exposure counter on your camera should indicate 24 or 36, depending on the length of the roll of film you shot. In addition, the camera's film-advance lever will no longer operate easily. The advance lever should never be forced because the film may be pulled out of its cassette inside the camera. If this happens, you will have to take the camera into a darkroom before opening it to unload the film.

Normally, you simply rewind the film into the light-tight cassette, unload the film in subdued light, and load another roll if you wish to continue shooting. To rewind the film, nearly every camera has a film rewind button or lever, which, when pressed, disengages the sprocket wheel so it can turn backwards. You then rewind the film by turning the rewind knob in the direction of the arrow marked on it. You should turn the knob until you feel a slight resistance and then wind

A Note on:

Sharpness

Both depth of field and shutter speed affect the sharpness of a negative, although in different ways. Depth of field controls the foreground to background sharpness—that is, which objects will be sharp and which won't. The shutter speed controls the effect of movement—that is, whether or not it will produce a blur.

The law of reciprocity implies that as you gain one type of sharpness, you lose the other (Figure 2.10). As you close down the aperture to gain depth of field, you must slow the shutter, thus losing the ability to freeze action. Conversely, if you speed up the shutter to decrease blur due to motion, you must open the aperture, thus collapsing the depth of field. The only ways to gain both depth of field and also faster shutter speeds are to increase the amount of light available or to use a faster film.

Some photographers, in an effort to increase sharpness, attempt to use slower, sharper film. It may work, but you shouldn't throw out your rolls of fast film too soon. While it is true that slower films generally are capable of producing finer detail, there must be enough light to expose them. Ironically, if light levels are low, the increased sharpness of the slower film may be lost on a blurred image or one with inadequate depth of field. On the other hand, although you can use faster shutter speeds and smaller apertures with faster films, the film its elf may not be capable of adequately recording the extra sharpness. In the end, you can produce increased sharpness on all fronts only by increasing the amount of light available to expose the negative.

past the resistance to pull the beginning of the film off the take-up reel and into the cassette. Unless you plan to process the film immediately, it is a good idea to return the cassette to the canister it came in and store it in a cool, dry place.

Sometimes, you may want to leave a bit of film extending from the cassette. In this case, you stop rewinding immediately after you feel the film come loose from the take-up reel. This trick can be handy if you do not finish a roll of film and want to be able to reload it later. You should mark the number of frames already shot on the leader extending from the cassette with a grease pencil for reference. If you plan on using this trick, it is a good idea to get in the habit of rewinding completed film all the way inside the cassette. That makes it easy to tell which rolls of film have been fully shot and which haven't. (It's very embarrassing to shoot the same roll twice and not nearly as economical as it sounds.)

FIGURE 2.10. Trading off depth of field for shutter speed

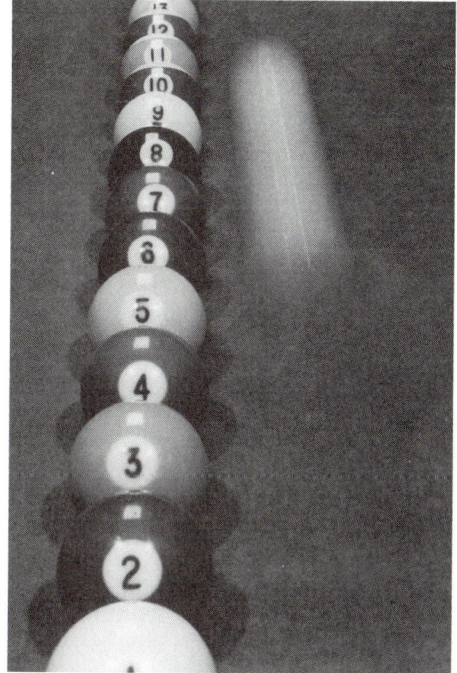

A. f/32 at 1/4 of a second   B. f/4 at 1/250 of a second

Using a Light Meter

Some light meters are built into cameras; others must be held separately. Whatever their physical appearance, light meters have one purpose: They determine the exposure settings (aperture and shutter speed) needed to record a usable image on film.

Light meters are of two types: reflected and incident. A **reflected light meter** is pointed at the subject to measure the amount of light reflected from the subject back toward the camera. An **incident light meter** is held in front of the subject, but facing the light source, to measure the light falling on the subject.

Nearly all meters built into cameras are of the reflected type. In order to use a reflected light meter effectively, you should be aware of its personality. A reflected light meter expects to look at a subject that is an "average gray." Although that sounds informal and approximate, **average gray** is a precisely defined photographic term; it represents 18 percent reflectance of the light that falls on a subject. You can even buy a photographic **gray card**—one that reflects 18 percent gray—to use as a meter target if you need to make exact exposure measurements. However, most subjects are very close to average and do reflect something like 18 percent of the light that hits them.

**FIGURE 2.11
Incorrect use of a
light meter**

A. Meter pointed skyward

B. Underexposed negative and dark
photo

If the meter gets fooled, it's usually because not all the light coming toward it
is reflected light. That is, it's because the meter is looking directly at a light *#16*
source of some kind, rather than at the indirect light reflected off the subject.
Figure 2.11 shows the wrong way and Figure 2.12 the right way to use a light
meter.

The problem of backlighting

A backlit subject is one where the light coming from behind the subject is as
strong or stronger than the light falling on the front of the subject. It could be
someone standing against a bright window, or a subject with the sun setting

**FIGURE 2.12
Correct use of
a light meter**

A. Meter pointed at subject

B. Properly exposed negative and
usable photo

behind it. The meter expects only reflected light, but primarily picks up the light from behind the subject. In effect, the meter "thinks" there is more light reflected from the subject than there really is. As a result, the meter indicates settings that are less than needed for proper exposure. The subject comes out too dark, perhaps even as a silhouette. The picture is underexposed.

Backlighting can be dealt with in several ways. In general, you want to avoid pointing the meter at anything except subject matter that reflects light. If the backlight is due to an expanse of bright sky behind the subject, you may be able to point the meter downward. In other cases, you may be able to move in very close to the subject so the meter avoids reading the backlight. If you can't get close to the subject, you may be able to use a technique called "substitute metering"—that is, pointing your meter at a substitute subject that receives the same front light as the subject, but one that allows you to avoid metering the backlight.

A convenient substitute subject is a gray card, or you can even use your hand. But because skin doesn't reflect the same as a gray card, you will need to make a correction. For dark skin, you meter the back of the hand and then close down one stop. You can remember to close down by noting that your thumb will point down when you hold the back of your hand toward you. For light skin, you meter the palm of the hand and open up one stop; your thumb will point upward as you hold the palm of your hand toward you. In any case, once the meter reading is made from a substitute subject and the exposure controls are set, you can reframe the picture the way you want and shoot.

Some types of reflected light meters deal better with backlighting than others. Built-in meters differ in what part of the scene they take exposure information from: **Averaging meters** consider the entire viewfinder frame; **spot meters** read only a small area in the center of the viewfinder; and **center-weighted meters** give most attention to the center area, although they don't entirely ignore the edges of the frame.

Spot and center-weighted meters are more likely to give correct exposures in backlight than averaging meters because both tend to ignore the backlight itself. You should know which type of meter your camera has so you can use it effectively. But keep in mind that no meter is foolproof. It has to be used with intelligence and with its limitations in mind.

Exposure Meter Modes

Three metering modes are in common use today in cameras with built-in meters: manual, automatic, and programmed.

In a manual exposure camera, you set both the shutter speed and aperture. Your camera's meter will usually have some sort of indicator inside the viewfinder that tells you whether the shutter speed-aperture combination you've selected will yield a correct exposure. If it shows under- or over-exposure, you adjust either the aperture or shutter speed until the indicator shows the exposure will be correct. The manual approach gives you complete control over exposure, but it also makes it easy to make exposure errors by setting the shutter or aperture incorrectly.

When using the automatic exposure mode, you select either the shutter speed or the aperture, and the camera automatically selects the other to produce a correct exposure. In an **aperture priority** system, you select the aperture and the camera automatically sets whatever shutter speed is needed to yield a correct exposure. In a **shutter priority** system, you set the shutter speed and the camera sets the aperture accordingly. In theory, a shutter priority system would be of most value when photographing action because you would be able to select a fast shutter speed to freeze the action, while the metering system would select whatever aperture was needed for accurate exposure. On the other hand, an aperture priority system would theoretically be of most value when depth-of-field considerations outweigh the need to stop action. In practice, both systems are flexible enough to accommodate nearly all shooting situations because, while you have direct control over only one of the two exposure controls, you also have indirect control over the other. For instance, if you had an aperture priority camera and wanted to force a fast shutter speed, you would only need to select a wide open aperture setting (like f/1.4). The exposure system would then be forced to select the fastest shutter speed possible for the film and lighting conditions.

A programmed exposure camera selects both the aperture and shutter speed based on a table of exposure settings stored electronically within the camera. Once you've selected a certain speed film to use, the programmed system measures the light available for exposure and automatically selects a certain aperture and shutter speed combination. Figure 2.13 shows a typical program

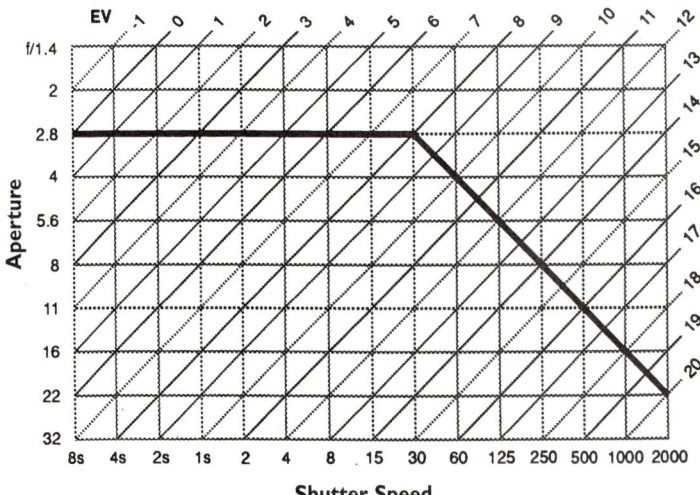

FIGURE 2.13.
Example exposure program for an f/2.8 lens used with ISO 100 film

FIGURE 2.14 Bracketing exposures

A. Negative strip showing (left to right) correct exposure, one stop overexposed, and one stop underexposed

B. Proof print of bracketed negatives

for an f/2.8 lens used with an ISO 100 film. When light levels are very low (EV-1 through EV8), the exposure system keeps the lens aperture wide open so as to use the fastest possible shutter speed. At higher light levels (EV9 through EV20), the exposure system gradually speeds up the shutter and closes the aperture to improve overall sharpness. Many programmed exposure cameras contain more than one program, each tailor-made to suit a given shooting situation. One program might maximize depth of field for shooting still-life subjects, while another would use the fastest possible shutter speed when shooting action.

Many cameras will give you a choice among several metering modes. You'll learn more about exposure if you work in the manual mode until you become familiar with the basics of metering and exposure. After that, you'll know when it's safe to let your camera make some or all of your exposure decisions for you.

Bracketing exposures

There will be times, despite your equipment and your intelligence, when you just cannot be certain of exposure. That's when you guess. But photographers have a special name for it: **bracketing,** which means taking the same shot at several exposure settings as insurance against incorrect exposure.

When you bracket an exposure, you guess systematically (Figure 2.14). You take the first shot at the exposure you think is correct. Then you take a second picture, but overexpose it. Finally you take a third shot that is underexposed. If you are using black and white film, you will probably want to bracket in full stops. That is, if your first exposure is f/5.6 at 1/125, then your second might be f/4 at 1/125 (overexposed a stop), and the third might be f/8 at 1/125 (underexposed a stop).

When you bracket, the hope, of course, is that one of the exposures will be correct. But don't let bracketing become a substitute for careful exposure measurement. It can help when the lighting is tricky, but it costs a lot of film and obviously won't work if you are shooting something spontaneous. Imagine trying to bracket as you are taking pictures of a football game.

How to

Operate a Camera

Step 1: Check to make sure there is no film in the camera by turning the rewind knob in the direction of the arrow marked on it. If the knob turns freely several times, the camera is empty and safe to open.

Step 2: In subdued light or shade, open the back of the camera and pull out the rewind knob. Remove the roll of film from its canister and insert the cassette in the left side of the camera.

Step 3: Push down the film rewind knob to lock the cassette in place, and draw the film across to the take-up reel by pulling the narrow end of the film. Insert the end of the film into the slit of the take-up reel.

Step 4: Make sure the holes along the edges of the film engage the sprocket wheel next to the take-up reel.

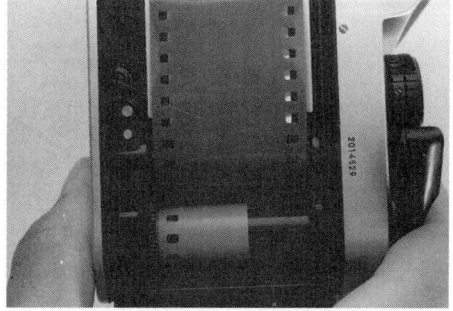

How to

Operate a Camera

Step 5: Close the camera back and turn the rewind knob in the direction of the arrow to take the slack out of the film.

Step 6: Shoot off two or three waste exposures to see whether the film is advancing properly. The rewind knob should turn backwards.

Step 7: Make certain your light meter is set for the correct ISO index for the film you are using.

Step 8: Take a meter reading and set the aperture accordingly.

How to

Operate a Camera

Step 9: Set the shutter speed. Both aperture and shutter speed should be set according to the reflected light reading made with your camera s meter.

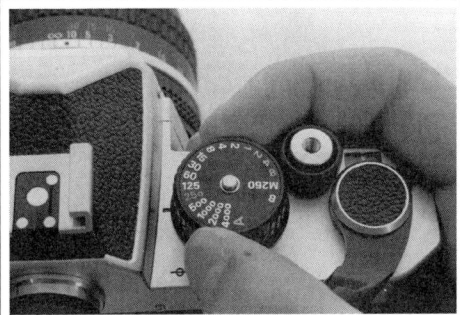

Step 10: Focus your camera on the subject.

Step 11: Release the shutter smoothly.

Step 12: Advance the film.

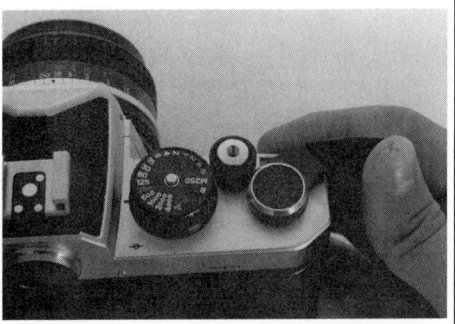

How to

Operate a Camera

Step 13: At the end of the roll, be careful not to pull the film out of the cassette. The film advance will be difficult to move, and the film counter should indicate that 24 or 36 exposures have been shot.

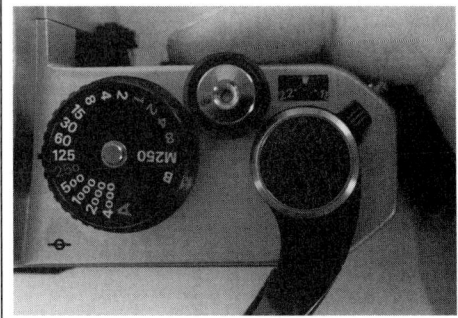

Step 14: Press the rewind button (usually on the bottom of the camera) to disengage the sprocket wheel.

Step 15: Rewind the film into its cassette using the rewind knob. When the film is nearly rewound, you will feel a slight resistance; wind past that point to pull the film completely inside the cassette.

Step 16: In subdued light or shade, open the back of the camera and remove the cassette.

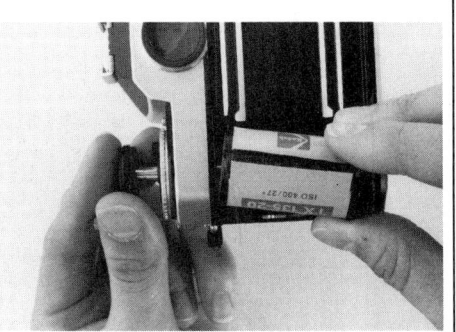

What Can
Go Wrong

Even experienced photographers occasionally have problems operating their cameras. Sometimes it is the fault of the camera; more often, it is the fault of the photographer.

Problem 1: Image out of focus

An out-of-focus shot can usually be distinguished from other blurred shots because often some area just in front or just behind the subject will be sharp.

Probable Cause:

You probably have not concentrated on focusing your camera carefully enough.

Solution:

Be more careful in focusing your camera for each shot. If the problem persists, it may be due to an out-of-adjustment viewfinder.

Problem 2:
Film with light streaks

Light streaks or fogged areas on film.

Probable Cause:

You may have opened the camera back before the film was rewound into the cassette (in which case, the fogged areas will form stripes across the width of the film), or you might have a faulty shutter, a damaged film cassette, or a camera back that doesn't close properly.

Solution:

Make sure the camera back is closed properly or, in the case of the other problems noted above, proper repairs are made.

What Can
Go Wrong

Problem 3: Blank film

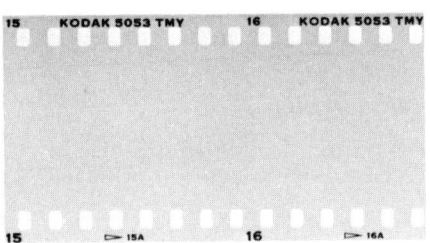

Probable Cause:

Film not exposed in camera, probably because it was misloaded and did not advance between exposures. Note that this is not a processing error. The visible film edge numbers indicate that the film was developed properly.

Solution:

Be sure to check the rewind knob as you advance the film to make sure it is turning backwards.

Problem 4: Blurred picture

Probable Cause:

The subject or camera moved during the exposure, and the shutter speed was too slow.

Solution:

Make sure you have the proper setting to freeze the image on film.

Problem 5: Double exposure

Two images appearing on the negative, one on top of the other.

Probable Cause:

You have not advanced the film between each shot.

Solution:

Be sure to advance the film between each shot if you do not have a camera with built-in protection against unintentional double exposure.

REVIEW
Questions

1. Why is speed important in selecting a film?

2. What is the important thing to remember in loading film into a 35 mm camera?

3. What does the aperture do and why is shutter speed important?

4. What is the law of reciprocity?

5. What are the points to remember in recording motion by a still camera?

6. How does a photographer achieve sharpness before taking a picture?

7. When do you unload the film in your camera?

8. What are the two kinds of light meters and how will they improve your photos?

9. What is backlighting and why is it sometimes a problem?

10. What is bracketing and how will it improve your photos?

CHAPTER THREE

SHOOTING FOR
Composition

Untitled
(Proposed Illustration for *The Bridge: Skyscrapers in Manhattan*) by Walker Evans, 1929.

SHOOTING FOR
Composition

Untitled

(Proposed Illustration for The Bridge; Skyscrapers in Manhattan) by Walker Evans, 1929

(Gelatin Silver Print 9.2 x 5.6 cm, Gift of Arnold Crane, 1970.917. Photograph ©1995,
The Art Institute of Chicago. All Rights Reserved)

Before he became a noted documentary photographer, Walker Evans had studied
design in Europe. This photo reveals his early interest in photographing real things in
abstract ways—where an iron fire escape in shadow and building windows in sunlight
result in an unusual photo that could be a painting. This work also illustrates the
importance of composition for the subject of any photo: the lines, rectangles and mesh
grates are rigid and irregular at the same time.

A GOOD PHOTOGRAPHER must know more than what dials to set and what knobs to turn. A good photographer has to visualize a scene and realize that it contains a photograph long before snapping the shutter to record a subject on film. Some people are born with an "eye" for photography, but most have to learn it—by taking pictures, by analyzing them, and by taking more pictures.

There are no simple absolutes to guide the search for effective photographs. The process begins simply with knowing how to hold the camera properly. From there, it goes to effectively "working the subject"—that is, visually exploring a subject with a camera. And, finally, it involves putting the guidelines for good composition into practice.

THREE

Using the Camera

From an elementary point of view, taking a picture requires that you know how to hold a camera and how to snap the shutter. Taking a good picture is a bit more complicated, but these two basics provide a good place to begin.

Hold the camera properly. Holding a camera is more than supporting the camera body in your hand. You should hold it in such a way that you can operate all essential controls without removing your eye from the viewfinder.

The proper way to hold a 35 mm camera is to cradle the lens and base of the camera body in the palm of your left hand. You should be able to operate both the aperture and focusing rings with your left hand. Your right hand grips the right side of the camera body in such a way that you can press the shutter release with your forefinger and work the film advance lever with your thumb. When necessary, you should also be able to operate the shutter speed dial with the thumb and forefinger of your right hand. This camera position is used to take horizontal photographs.

To take vertical pictures, most people simply turn the camera 90 degrees counterclockwise. Your right hand still grips the side of the camera, but it's positioned above. Your left hand cradles the lens and left side of the camera, now positioned below. You should still be able to work the camera controls without taking your eye from the viewfinder.

Steady the camera while you shoot. Steadying the camera while you shoot can eliminate blurred pictures. For most shots, you can brace the camera by tucking your left arm in against your body and gently pressing the camera back against your cheek and forehead. You can also use the neck strap of the camera to help you steady it by getting your hands inside of the strap or by wrapping the strap around one wrist several times. By turning that wrist, you can place tension on the strap around the back of your neck.

If you are using particularly slow shutter speeds, you should try to find a support to help you keep the camera from moving. You can lean up against a wall, for example, or support your elbows on a table. If you are sitting on the ground, you can place your elbows on your knees. At slow shutter speeds, the steadier you can hold the camera, the sharper your pictures will be.

For all types of shots, it's a good idea to practice holding the camera until you arrive at a posture that is both steady and comfortable for you. You can even look at yourself in a mirror to see whether your arms, hands, and fingers are positioned properly.

Snap the shutter properly. "Snapping" the shutter is not as mundane as it sounds. Actually, it is better to think more in terms of pressing or squeezing the shutter, rather than snapping it. Those words suggest more of a deliberate gentleness, but whoever heard of "press-shots" or "squeeze-shots"? Still, you shouldn't punch down on the shutter release. When you're ready to take a picture, you should be relaxed: Take careful aim, take a breath and release it, hold very still, and press down on the shutter release smoothly and firmly. Jabbing or jerking the release button may cause you to move the camera and blur the photo.

If you are using slow shutter speeds, you should place your right thumb under the camera, then squeeze thumb and shutter-finger together. Your thumb will counterbalance the movement of your forefinger and help prevent camera movement.

Working the Subject

You should never worry about making every frame a masterpiece. One of the advantages of the 35 mm camera is that you can take many photographs on one roll of film. Your camera should be used as something of an exploratory device— as a scratch pad, as some photographers call it. If you take but one frame of each subject you encounter, chances are you will wind up with nothing worth printing. When you use a 35 mm camera, you need to be able to recognize that a scene or situation has the potential for a successful photograph. Once you decide that, you can begin "working" the subject—exploring it with your camera (Figure 3.1).

Change your proximity to the subject. You can think of yourself as a film director developing a scene. A movie scene frequently begins with a long, overall shot to establish the general location. After that, the camera often moves in for a medium shot, concentrating on the subject of interest. Then, it usually comes in for a tight close-up. You can do much the same thing by circling around the subject from a distance, watching for effective lighting and visually interesting backgrounds. When you make your long shots, you will want to be careful to avoid backgrounds that are cluttered and that distract from the subject. As you move in closer, still circling, you continue shooting photographs each time you see something that looks like it may work. Eventually, you get in tight on the subject, so it fills the frame completely if possible.

Closing in on the subject is important. If there is a single common error by beginning photographers, it is that they take their photographs from too far away. As a result, the viewer can't see the subject well because it's too small. At

FIGURE 3.1. "Working" the subject by changing proximity and angles

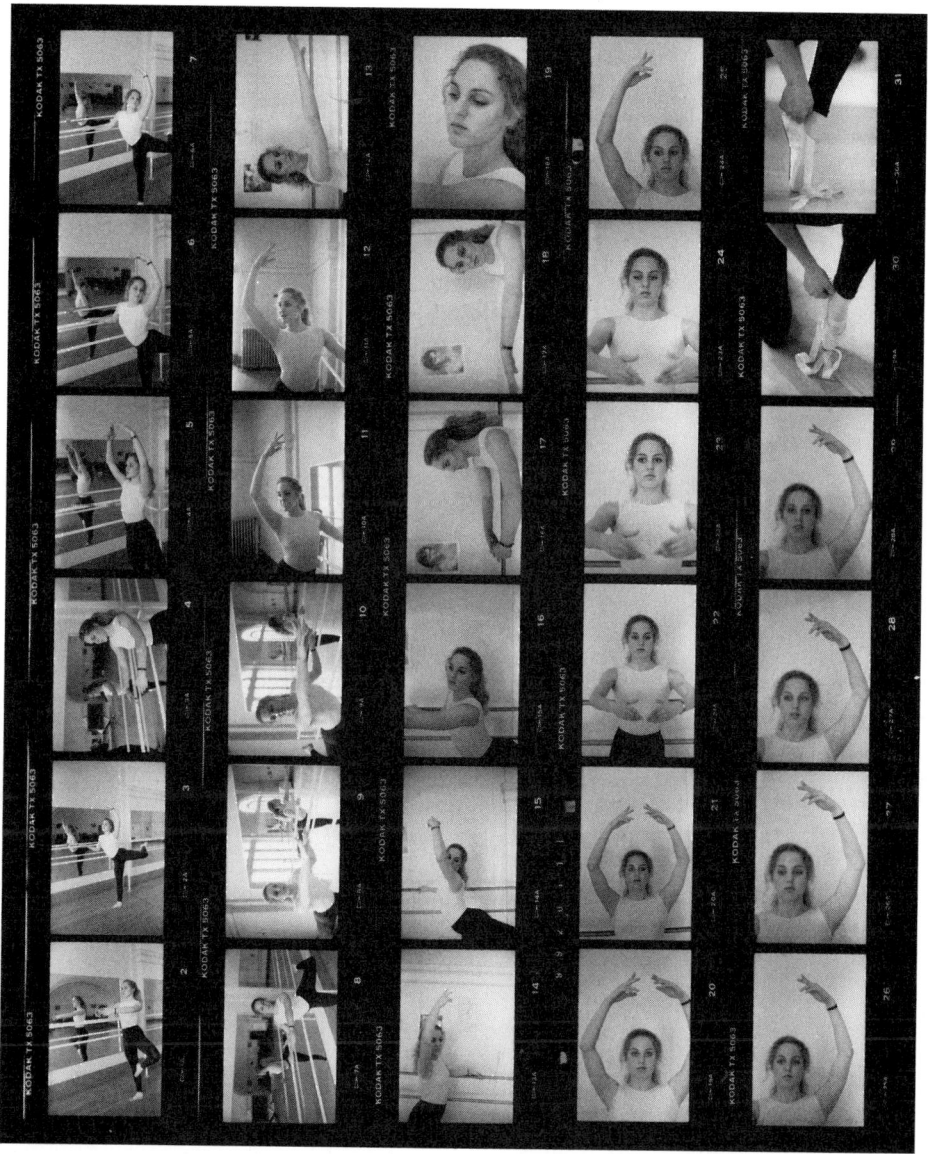

the same time, many distracting details creep in to compete with the subject for attention. You can always improve your photographs by getting closer.

Vary your vantage point. While you are moving in on the subject, vary your vantage point. Shoot from high and low angles, always looking for the interesting angle. The vast majority of photographs are taken from eye-level. But that's the way we all look at the world anyway. Your pictures will be more interesting if you try to find something fresher: Try bird's eye views and worm's eye views. You can climb up on things and get down on the ground. It's good exercise—and often leads to good photographs.

Keep your subjects occupied. When you are taking pictures of people, you will get stronger photographs if you give them props to work with. Having something to do will help them relax. A prop can be anything that fits the person and the picture: a flower, a hat, a book.

Frame your subject tightly. You will also have stronger pictures if you eliminate unessential backgrounds by framing tightly—that is, by including the subject alone in the frame of the viewfinder. If you do include backgrounds, they should complement the subject and help tell the story. For instance, a portrait of a painter beside one of her paintings tells a story on two levels. We see what she looks like. At the same time, we are allowed a glimpse at her thought processes by studying the painting.

Avoid taking all pictures as horizontals. For some reason, that seems to be the most natural way to hold the camera when you're first getting started. But it's not the most effective frame for many subjects, including most portraits. If you're in doubt, you can shoot the picture both as a horizontal and a vertical.

Don't be afraid to experiment. You should always be willing to risk an occasional failure to see whether something will work. Later, when going through your shots after the film is processed, you can decide what worked well and what didn't.

Taking good photographs is a deliberate process of discovery. As you gain experience, you'll know better what angles won't work and which are more likely to yield results. You will be able to narrow down the field of experimentation and concentrate on strong possibilities. Eventually, you may arrive at the point where you are able to "previsualize" your photographs—that is, see the image in your mind's eye and then set about creating it in your camera.

It may comfort you to know that most professional photographers are satisfied if they get two or three successful photographs from a roll of film. If you find that you are getting many more than that, perhaps your standards are too low.

If you expect to grow as a photographer you will always need to experiment and try things you're not sure of. But you must be careful of sloppiness. No amount of experimentation is a justification of sloppy or haphazard shooting.

Principles of Composition

The title of this section is misleading—in fact, a lie. It is not going to list any principles of composition.

Photographic composition has been aptly defined as the strongest way of seeing. You usually hear about composition in the form of a set of principles. But you really learn about composition by taking photographs, by studying them, and by taking more photographs. Eventually composition becomes second nature; it is simply incorporated into the way you see photographs. Edward Weston said it well: "To consult the rules of composition before taking a photograph is like consulting the laws of gravitation before taking a walk."

All of this isn't to say that composition is unimportant, but rather that it is not usually in the forefront of your mind as you photograph. Composition, the design of the photograph, is crucial. It lies at the center of photography as a visual form. While there is a fairly well recognized set of principles for analyzing composition—concerning things like balance, contrast, proportion—they tend to be useful primarily after the photograph is made. What we have here is a set of guidelines and shooting strategies that should assist you in strengthening your own compositions as you shoot. To make them a little more interesting, we've overstated them as absolutes. As rules, all of them ache to be broken at one time or another. As guidelines, you can take them as a challenge to strengthen your photographic eye and personal style.

The key to a strong image lies in its simplicity. There should be nothing in the photograph that doesn't contribute to its overall quality (Figure 3.2). This isn't to say that a photograph must be simplistic, but that all its elements must add up to something coherent. You must always be on guard against backgrounds that distract, subjects that compete, and inclusion of the extraneous and unessential.

FIGURE 3.2. Keeping the shot simple

A. Busy background and loose framing distract from portrait

B. Simpler background and tighter composition enhance portrait

Every photograph must have a central subject or a focal point. Even when you have more than one person or object, you can achieve a good photo by developing a "center of interest" around which to organize the picture. When you have a group of three or more, you should avoid arrangements that waste space and look trite or static. Instead, you can keep your subjects close together and stagger the arrangement, overlapping them and varying the height. Giving the subjects something to do can also help to develop a strong focal point. Depth of field is another way to create a central focal point. By using it, you can keep your subject in focus and the foreground and background out of focus.

The center of interest is not always best placed in the center of the photograph. The center is graphically the weakest point in a rectangle. Stronger

FIGURE 3.3.
Establishing points of interest according to the "Rule of Thirds"

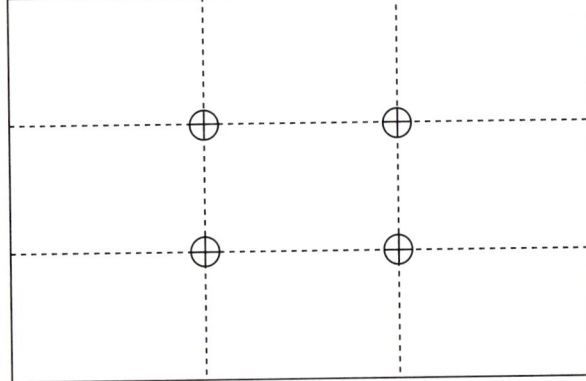

FIGURE 3.4.
Composing by the "Rule of Thirds"

(Photo by Chris Johns; published with permission)

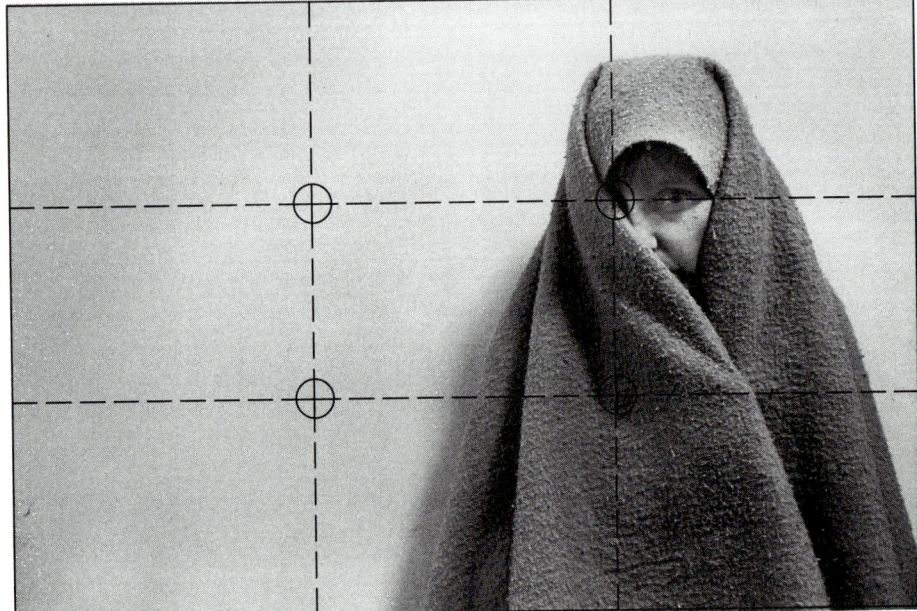

FIGURE 3.5. Using the corner to place the subject

(Photo by Randy Wood; published with permission)

THREE

points of placement are suggested by the **rule of thirds,** which means mentally dividing the rectangular frame of your photograph into thirds both horizontally and vertically and establishing four points where the imaginary dividing lines intersect (Figure 3.3). You can then place your center of interest at one of the four points (Figure 3.4). As an alternative and for a bit of surprise in your compositions, you can also try placing the center of interest in one of the corners (Figure 3.5).

Centering your subject is an easy trap to fall into because the focusing aid in your viewfinder is dead center in the frame. That makes it tempting to put the focusing aid over your subject, then focus and shoot. You can avoid the temptation by making focusing and framing two distinct steps in picture taking.

FIGURE 3.6. Comparison of centered and non-centered symmetrical subjects

Center symmetrical subjects. The rule of thirds is extremely useful for images that are asymmetrical, that is, images where shapes and patterns are not balanced around some central axis. And while you'll find that most images are indeed asymmetrical, you'll occasionally discover others that will yield the strongest images when treated as symmetrical patterns. In those cases, the photograph will usually work best if the subject is centered, thus enhancing its symmetrical appearance. Symmetrical composition often gives the photograph a formal tone. Compare the two renditions of the same subject in Figure 3.6.

Dominant lines help organize a photograph. A dominant line might be the edge of an object. It might be the horizon. It might be a stream winding its way through some rural scene. Dominant lines are useful because they can help establish points of interest or can give the photograph direction (Figure 3.7).

**FIGURE 3.7.
Establishing
dominant lines**

*(Photo by Randy Wood:
published with
permission)*

They can provide a kind of visual backbone that holds the rest of the photograph together. But a dominant line should not divide the picture in half: Halves and fourths are boring. Thirds are more interesting, but the ancient Greeks said the best proportion was the "golden section": roughly 3/5.

Be aware of subject-background relationships. When you've got a number of technical details on your mind—aperture, shutter speed, focus, etc.—and you're concentrating on getting what you want from your subject, it's easy to overlook the background. But in the final print, the background will be as much a part of the image as the subject. You need to train yourself to look past your subject in the viewfinder to study the background. You need to look into the far corners of the viewfinder as well as the center.

In general, you'll probably want the background to be as simple as it can be, but that doesn't mean the background should always be stark and bare. It depends on whether the background contributes or distracts from the meaning and graphic qualities of the photograph. If the background carries information that is essential to your image or helps create a striking visual image, then you'll want to keep it sharp and give it presence. But if the background just happens to be there or even distracts, then you'll want to make it as simple and unobtrusive as you can. You can resort to a number of strategies to simplify backgrounds. Probably the most effective is to get closer so your subject fills the frame and the background becomes a less significant part of the image. You can also make the depth of field shallower either by using a larger aperture, or by moving in closer, or by using a longer focal length if you're using a zoom lens or have more than one lens. You can often find simpler backgrounds merely by changing camera angles so you're shooting against the sky (north sky works best) or shooting against a grassy area or a plain wall.

You should also be aware of tonal relationships between subject and background. By putting a light subject against a dark background (Figure 3.8) you can emphasize the subject. You can, of course, accomplish the same thing by putting a dark subject against a light background. At the same time, there are images that work better when the subject and background are similar in tone.

You can also use the background as a frame for the subject. The background in a photograph is often called negative space. Large amounts of negative space can create dramatic compositions (Figure 3.9).

You'll generally want to keep subject and background distinct by avoiding what photographers call mergers. A **merger** is a confusing association of subject with background.

There's really no right or wrong in any of this. Sometimes mergers create fascinating images. Sometimes intricate backgrounds are successful. Sometimes large amounts of negative space weakens the composition. One thing is reasonably certain, however-your photographs will be stronger if you are aware of subject-background relationships as you shoot.

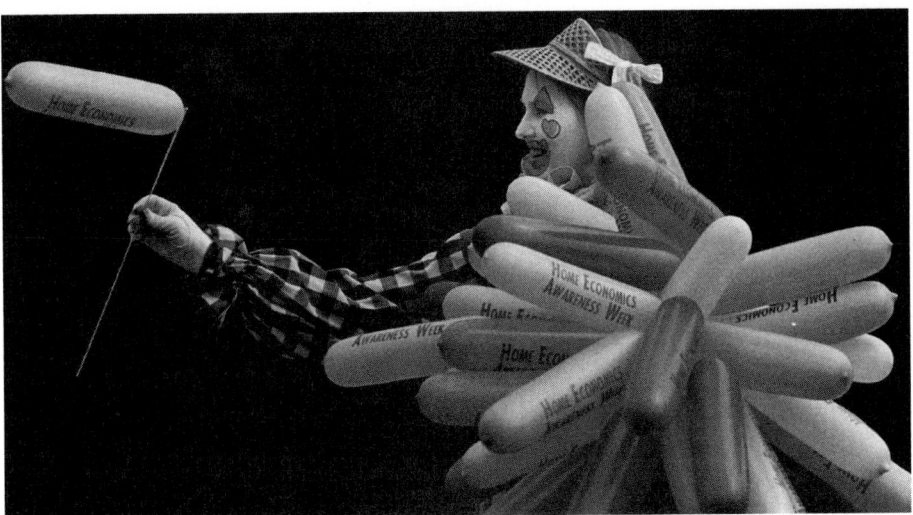

FIGURE 3.8.
Emphasizing by contrast
(Photo by Stuart Wong;
published with permission)

FIGURE 3.9. Use of
negative space to
create drama

In fact, there's nothing sacred about any of these guidelines for creating stronger composition. As you photograph, you'll almost certainly find ways to break the rules and create yet stronger compositions. The important thing is to develop an eye for organizing spatial relationships within the frame of the photograph. It is rare, however, that spatial relationships are the only thing you need to consider—a photograph is taken in time as well as space.

Beyond Saying "Cheese"

There is more to taking good photographs than successful camera operation and skilled composition. Certain psychological factors also come into play between the photographer and the person being photographed.

Your primary aim at this point is to get your subject to relax so you can take the photo. You can achieve a great deal by talking because that will put the person at ease. It helps to do some research beforehand so you will have something to talk about and won't be embarrassed by your ignorance. A running commentary about the weather, subjects of mutual interest, what you are doing as you take your photos, or even chatter like "a funny thing happened to me on the way to the photo session" are possibilities.

You can also put people at ease by giving them roles to play. This may be as simple as getting them to do something they normally do. For example, if you are taking a photograph of a potter, get him or her to make a pot. If this kind of thing is not possible, give your subject something to play with: a hat, an umbrella,

THREE

FIGURE 3.10.
"Decisive Moment"
(at a basketball game)
*(Photo by Stuart Wong;
published with permission)*

a ball, a hand puppet. This solves the problem of what to do with your subject's hands. Otherwise they will be folded or in pockets—and the results won't be good. If the prop is selected wisely, it can add a great deal to the photograph by stylizing it. Philippe Halsman, who shot more than one hundred covers for *Life* magazine, used to ask subjects to jump in place while he photographed them. He felt that having them do something helped subjects relax and avoid self-conscious poses.

Another thing helps in this regard. You should know the tricks of camera operation so well that you don't have to concentrate too much on lighting and settings. The shooting sequence then becomes something between two people and not two people and a camera.

A Note on

Timing

A photograph represents the scene in front of the camera—at the instant the shutter is released. For most subjects, some moments are more interesting than others. A strong photograph is the result of timing as well as an eye for composition. The French photographer Henri Cartier-Bresson called it the "Decisive Moment"—that single instant when objects within the frame organize themselves into a strong composition and also reveal something about themselves that is worth capturing on film (Figure 3.10).

A good photographer, catlike, stalks that moment. Sometimes, when things move quickly before the camera, it's a matter of reflex and instinct. You take pictures rapidly and deliberately, ready to pounce when that single revealing instant comes. Sometimes it's a matter of patience, of waiting in one spot long enough for the moment to arrive. You might be taking portraits, working your subjects and waiting for the moment when they finally begin to relax, let down their guard, and reveal themselves as they really are.

Sometimes you have absolute control and create the moment yourself. You might, for instance, be working in a studio creating a still-life, arranging and rearranging things, when suddenly you know you've got it. You may take lots of pictures in search of that moment, but when you finally get it, it will be The Picture on the roll. The ability to find moment photographs consistently is what distinguishes strong from weak photographers. The quest is what makes photography so fascinating.

How to

Take Pictures

Step 1: Cradle the camera in your left hand so that you can operate both the focusing and aperture rings. Grip the right side of the camera with your right hand. You should be able to operate the shutter speed dial, the shutter release, and the film advance lever without taking your eye from the viewfinder.

Step 2: For horizontals, gently press the top of the camera against your forehead. Brace your left elbow against your body and use the camera strap for additional rigidity.

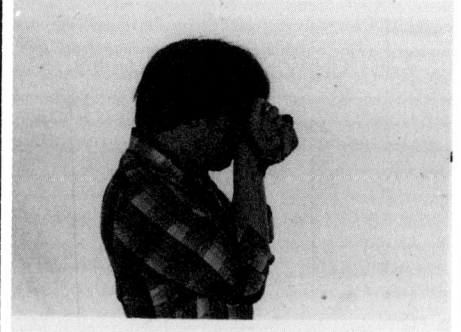

Step 3: For verticals, cradle the left side of the camera in your left hand. The right side of the camera, positioned upward, is pressed gently into your forehead. Sometimes, the strap can be used for additional support.

Step 4A: Seek additional support to keep the camera steady if you are using slow shutter speeds. Brace yourself against a wall

THREE

How to

Take Pictures

Step 4B:
or, place your elbows on a table

Step 4C:
or, sit on the ground and place your elbows on your knees.

Step 5: Make a meter reading, being careful to avoid stray light sources or backlight. If needed, make a meter reading off your hand and open up one stop.

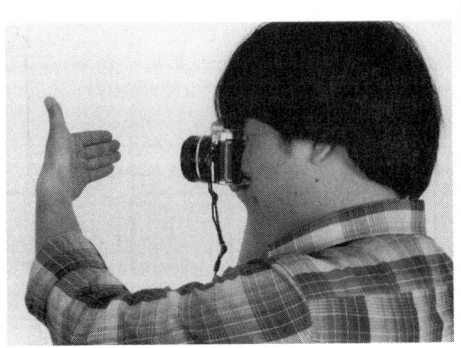

Step 6: Set the aperture and shutter speed according to the meter reading.

How to

Take Pictures

Step 7: Focus carefully on the subject. Then frame the photograph, perhaps according to the "rule of thirds."

Step 8: Release the shutter to take the picture, making sure to squeeze and not jerk the camera.

Step 9: Work the subject. Start back with long shots. . .

Step 10: . . .and then move in for close-ups.

THREE

How to

Take Pictures

Step 11: Try different vantage points. Try some shots from high angles. . .

Step 12: . . .and some from low angles.

What Can
Go Wrong

Experience will eliminate most of the common mistakes you might make early in your photographic career. This guide should help you eliminate them quickly.

THREE

Problem 1:
Tilted horizontal line

Probable Cause:

You probably tilted the camera when you took the picture.

Solution:

Make sure the back of the camera is parallel to the ground or to the horizontal plane of objects.

Problem 2 (A):
Subject too small in picture

Probable Cause:

You are not close enough to your subject.

Solution (B):

Get closer; use a telephoto lens if necessary.

A. Problem print

B. Solution Print

What Can
Go Wrong

Problem 3 (A): Subject lost in photograph

Probable Cause:

You were not careful in selecting the background.

Solution (B):

Frame the subject tightly, and throw the surrounding area out of focus by limiting the depth of field.

A. Problem Print

B. Solution Print

Problem 4: Subject distorted: Wrong lens used

Probable Cause:

You shot the picture too close with a normal or wide angle lens.

Solution:

Move back or use a telephoto lens.

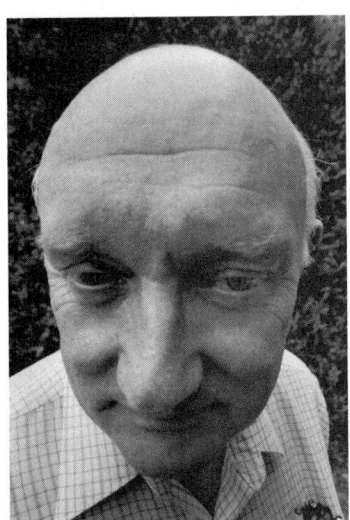

What Can
Go Wrong

Problem 5 (A): Trite group shots

Probable Cause:

The subjects are arranged awkwardly or statically, and space is wasted.

Solution (B):

Move your subjects closer together, stagger the arrangement, and, if possible, give them something to do.

A. Problem Print

B. Solution Print

REVIEW
Questions

1. What are the important things to remember in using a camera?

2. What is meant by "working the subject?"

3. Is it best to get close to your subject, or far away?

4. How should you "frame" your subject?

5. Should all your photos be horizontals? Why not?

6. Is experimentation in photography important? Why?

7. What are the main factors in photo composition?

8. What is the "Rule of Thirds" and how does it improve the composition of a photo?

9. What are "dominant lines?"

10. How can a photographer put a subject at ease?

Developing
and
Printing

"The contemplation of things as they are, without error, without substitution or imposture, is in itself, a nobler thing than a whole harvest of invention."

Francis Bacon

**—Quotation from Francis Bacon pinned to
Dorothea Lange's darkroom door, circa 1930s**

P · A · R · T

TWO
2

Developing and Printing

"The contemplation of things as they are, without error, without substitution or imposture, is in itself a nobler thing than a whole harvest of invention."

Francis Bacon

—Quotation from Francis Bacon pinned to
Dorothea Lange's darkroom door, circa 1930s

CHAPTER FOUR

DEVELOPING
The Film

"Normandy Invasion" by Robert Capa, 1944

DEVELOPING
The Film

"Normandy Invasion" by Robert Capa, 1944
(© 1944 Robert Capa and Magnum Photos, Inc. Published with permission)

Robert Capa covered the wars in China and Spain from 1935 to 1940 for various European magazines and the North African and Italian campaigns for *Life*, before being selected as one of four photographers to accompany the first troops going ashore in the invasion of France in June 1944. As Capa ran down the ramp, bullets tore holes in the waist-deep, cold water around him. "It was still very early and very gray for good pictures," he later wrote, "but the gray water and the gray sky made the little men dodging the surrealistic designs for Hitler's anti-invasion brain trust, very effective."

He shot film for an hour and a half, then returned to Portsmouth where it was sent to London. There, in a rush to process the film quickly, a technician put the negative in the dryer with the heat on high and closed the door. With no air circulating, the film emulsion melted. Of the 72 images on the two rolls of 35 mm film Capa had shot during the landing, only 11 pictures were printable. These were slightly blurred, however, like the one reproduced in this chapter. In its caption, *Life* noted that Capa had moved his camera in the "excitement of the moment." He did not learn the truth until he returned to London in July.

Always dismissive of his own personal safety, Capa once said, "If your pictures aren't good enough, you're not close enough." He was killed by a land mine in Indochina in 1954.

WHEN YOU TAKE A PHOTOGRAPH, the film is exposed to light and forms a **latent image**—an image that is not visible to the eye, but that can be developed to make it visible. During development, that latent image is made both visible and permanent by converting it into a negative that can be used to make positive prints.

In some ways, developing negatives is the most crucial step in the photographic process. Developing errors are difficult or impossible to correct later on. A bad negative will probably have to be reshot (if that is possible) or discarded altogether. There is no substitute for a good negative, one that is properly exposed and developed.

FOUR

Light-Sensitive Properties of Film

Film records its images because of its light sensitivities. It is able to do so because of its structure and other factors: speed and grain structure, color sensitivity, and contrast.

Structure of film

Black-and-white film is a sandwich of four primary layers (Figure 4.1). The photographically active layer is the **emulsion,** which consists of light-sensitive silver salts, or silver halide crystals, suspended in transparent gelatin. The emulsion is coated with a **scratch-resistant substance** to prevent abrasion in handling. The emulsion is fixed onto a transparent plastic film base, usually cellulose-acetate in modern film. The backside of the **film base,** opposite the emulsion, is coated with an **antihalation layer,** designed to keep light rays from being reflected back up through the film base and exposing the emulsion a second time.

Film reaction to light

The most important ingredient in photographic film is the light-sensitive silver salts in the emulsion. The silver salts are actually silver halide crystals, which include silver chloride, silver iodide, or silver bromide. During exposure of the film, a few of the silver ions in the crystals that are exposed to light are selectively converted into metallic silver atoms. However, no silver ions in the

FIGURE 4.1.The structure of black and white film

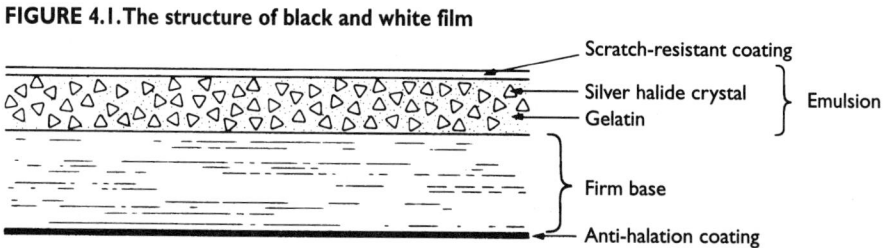

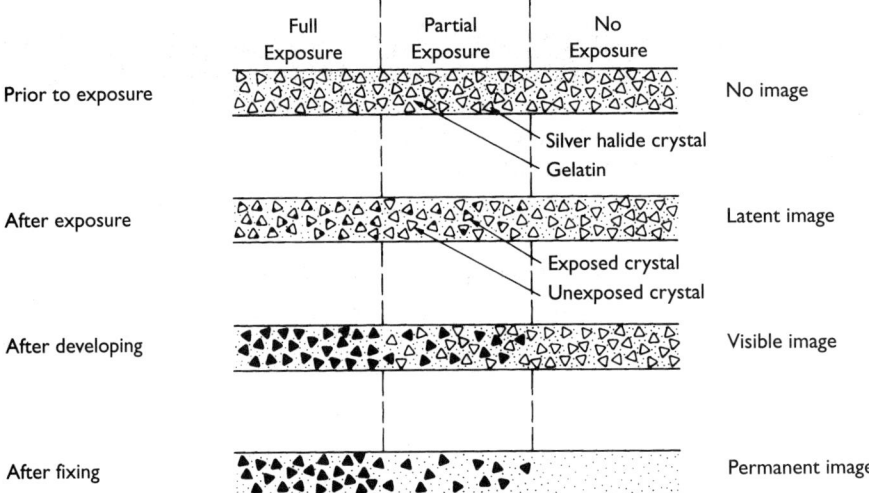

FIGURE 4.2. Film stages from exposure through fixing the image

crystals that aren't exposed to light are converted to metallic silver. The degree of exposure—the amount of light that reaches the emulsion—determines the number of silver crystals converted to metallic silver.

When a silver halide crystal is exposed to light, only a few of the silver ions in the crystal are converted to metallic silver atoms (Figure 4.2). At this stage, the image on the film is invisible—that is, it is a **latent image.** Not enough silver ions have been converted to make a **visible image.** But the few metallic silver atoms make it possible for the developer to "recognize" exposed crystals during processing and convert the remaining silver ions in them to metallic silver. Developing, then, greatly magnifies the effect of exposure and makes the latent image visible. Unexposed silver crystals, which contain no metallic silver atoms, are left unchanged by the developer because they contain only ions and no metallic silver that the developer recognizes. During fixing, the unexposed crystals are removed from the emulsion. At this stage, the image is not only visible from the action of the developer, but it is also permanent because the fixer removes the unexposed and still light-sensitive crystals from the emulsion.

**FIGURE 4.3.
Granular structure of
slow and fast films**

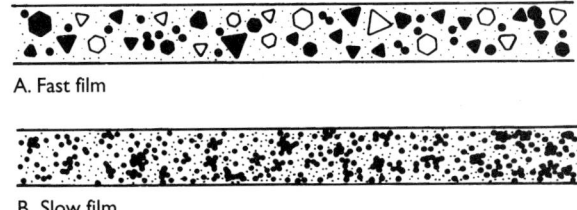

A. Fast film

B. Slow film

Characteristics of film

• **Speed.** Black-and-white films differ principally in the size of the silver halide crystals in their emulsions (Figure 4.3). Generally, the larger the size of the crystals, the more light-sensitive (or faster) the film is. The higher the film's speed rating, the larger the silver halide crystals in the film's emulsion.

But the increase in speed is not without trade-offs. Because the image-recording substance—the silver halide crystal—is coarser, the film cannot record as much detail as a slower film with finer crystals. Fast films are not as sharp as slow films. Also, when fast films are enlarged, they tend to have a speckled, or grainy, appearance. The prominence of the grain pattern depends on the degree of enlargement as well as the size of the silver halide crystals. The important point is that you gain in light sensitivity as you move from a slower to a faster film, but you lose in ability to record extremely fine detail.

• **Color sensitivity.** Most common black-and-white films are **panchromatic**—that is, sensitive to about the same colors of light as those seen by the human eye. Silver halide crystals themselves are sensitive only to blue light. Film manufacturers add sensitizers to panchromatic films to extend the sensitivity to include green and red light also. Some films contain additional sensitizers to make them sensitive to infrared light, which is not visible to the human eye. These emulsions, aptly named **infrared films,** are useful for haze penetration (haze does not scatter infrared as much as visible light) and for special effects. They also have scientific applications.

• **Gradation of tone.** Most films are designed to render a series of tones, or shades of gray, from black to white. When you don't want such gradations of tones but prefer blacks and whites only, you can select a film that gives high contrast. A **high-contrast film,** usually used with special developing chemicals, records only blacks and whites with no shades of gray in between. This type of film is useful in photographing line work, like the type on this page, where tonal shading is undesirable. High-contrast films can also be used to create interesting special effects. When used to record a normal scene, they drop out gray tones and render the scene as shades of black and white.

Chemicals and Basic Equipment for Developing Film

Chemicals

You need to use a number of chemicals to develop film. These chemicals are: developer, stop bath, fixer, hypo clearing agent, and a wetting agent (Figure 4.4). These chemicals come in either powder or liquid form and must be mixed for use. To lengthen the life of the developer, it should be stored in dark brown glass

FOUR

FIGURE 4.4.
Chemicals to develop film: Developer, stop bath, fixer, hypo clearing agent, wetting agent

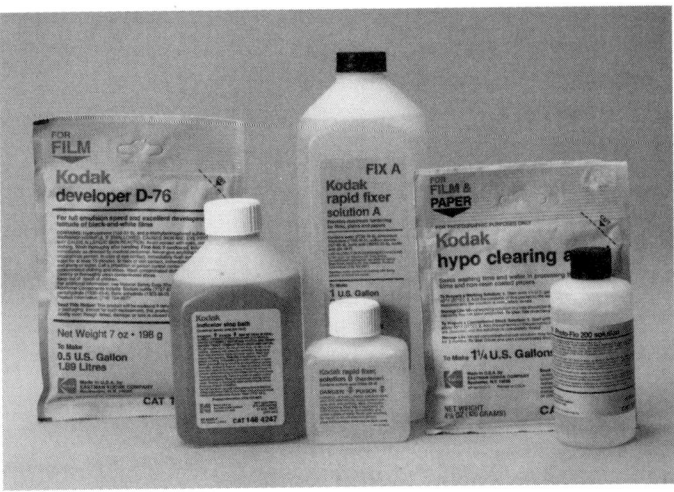

bottles or other containers that keep out light. To safeguard the environment and yourself, never pour any of these chemicals down the drain.

• **Developer.** A variety of developers in liquid and powder form are available (Figure 4.5). Typically, developers consist of a **developing agent** and several other chemicals that make the developer practical. The developing agent reduces the silver ions in the exposed silver halide crystals to metallic silver to make the latent image on the film visible. Since the developing agent acts slowly, practical developers also contain an **activator** that accelerates development by making the developer alkaline. This is why the developer feels "soapy"—soap too, is an alkaline substance. Practical developers also contain a **preservative,** which slows down oxidation, or spoilage, of the developing agent by air, and a **restrainer,** which helps keep the developing agent from converting unexposed silver ions into metallic silver atoms.

The two key ingredients in the developer are the developing agent and the activator, however. The developing agent does the actual work—it provides the "brains" by making the distinction between exposed and unexposed silver halide crystals. But the developer works too slowly to be practical and requires an activator—the "brawn" that reduces developing times from hours or even days to minutes.

The strength of the developing solution is important. Some types can be mixed to recommended strength and used according to the "one-shot" system. That is, the developer is used once and discarded. Other types can be used in a replenishing system in which fresh solution is added to a stock solution proportionate to the number of rolls that have been developed. Different developers also have different storage periods, so you should read the manufacturer's instructions carefully.

• **Stop bath.** Two types of stop bath are in common use. In one, fresh water is poured into the tank to dilute the developer and halt its action. In the other, a weak acid solution is used to chemically neutralize the developer. The water stop is the most common. Your film instructions will indicate if an acid stop bath is required. You should throw it away after one period of use.

• **Fixer.** This solution stabilizes, or fixes, the photographic image by removing unexposed silver halide crystals from the film emulsion. The formal chemical name for fixer is sodium thiosulfate, once known as sodium hyposulfate. Fixer is still often called by a shortened version, "hypo." It can be reused until it becomes exhausted. A testing solution is available to check whether the fixer is worn out or still working.

• **Hypo clearing agent.** This solution cuts down the time needed for washing the negatives by making the fixer, or hypo, more soluble in water. The storage life varies from type to type. Generally, the liquid types are mixed, used once, and discarded.

• **Wetting agent.** This solution helps the negatives to dry evenly and to eliminate water spotting. One such wetting agent is Kodak's Photo-Floe. Although it can be reused for several times if you mix a large amount, it is best to discard it after each developing session.

FIGURE 4.5. Variety of developers

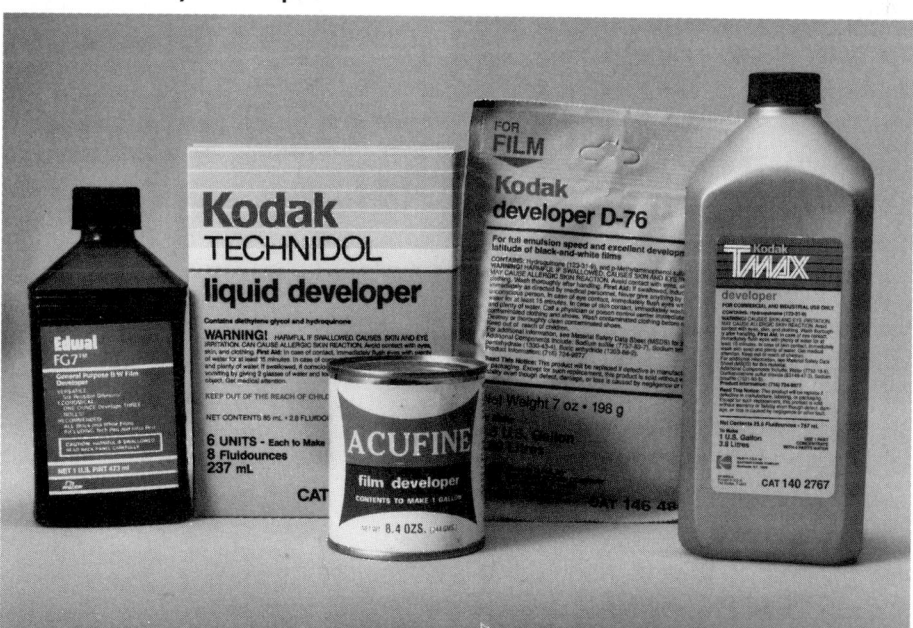

FIGURE 4.6. Developing tanks and reels: Plastic (left) and stainless steel (right)

Basic equipment

Any well-equipped darkroom must have a number of essential items of equipment. It is a good idea to buy high-quality, rustproof items that are made of plastic, stainless steel, or glass.

• **Developing tanks and reels** (Figure 4.6). The film goes on a reel and into the tank so it can be developed. Plastic reels and tanks are less expensive than stainless steel reels and tanks, and they are easier to get used to. Stainless steel tanks and reels, however, are more durable and once mastered, more efficient. Both plastic and stainless steel tanks can be purchased to hold a single reel or

FIGURE 4.7.
Other equipment
for developing film:
Can opener, scissors,
thermometer,
and timer

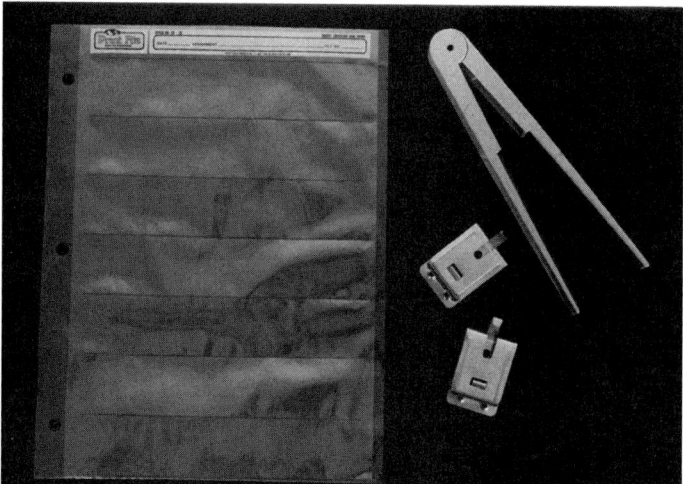

FIGURE 4.8.
Equipment used after developing: Squeegee tongs, film clips, and negative sleeves

several reels. Unless you frequently plan to develop several rolls of film at one time, a single-reel tank is adequate.

•   **Can opener and scissors** (Figure 4.7). The can opener is used not only to open the chemical containers, but to pry open the film cassette. The scissors are needed to cut the leader off the film before winding it onto the developing reel. They are also needed to cut the negatives into strips after they have dried.

•   **Thermometer and timer** (Figure 4.7). The thermometer enables you to test the temperature of chemicals and water. The timer gives you the correct time for all the various steps you must follow. A special photographic timer is best, but you can use your wristwatch if it has a sweep second hand.

•   **Squeegee tongs and film clips** (Figure 4.8). The squeegee tongs or a sponge help you remove excess water from both sides of the film before drying it. The film clips hold the film for drying. A film dryer is a piece of equipment designed to dry film in heated conditions. If you don't have a dryer, however, you can hang the film by the clips in any dust-free location for about one hour.

•   **Negative sleeves** (Figure 4.8). These cellophane or plastic holders protect your negatives from damage. By using fingernail clippers, you can put curved edges on the four corners of a negative strip, allowing for easier insertion of the negatives into the sleeve.

Processing the Film

Despite its importance, negative development is one of the simplest and most mechanical steps in photography. Once you have established your developing technique, there is no need for judgment. The secret to successful film developing is consistency and care. After you carefully establish a technique that yields good negatives for you, you will want to follow that technique consistently roll after roll.

- **Preparing the chemicals.** The first step in developing film is preparing the chemicals you need. The manufacturer's instructions should be followed when mixing the chemicals. Only appropriate containers, usually glass or plastic jugs, should be used. You should avoid using metal containers. After the chemicals are mixed, the containers for each of the solutions must be labeled and dated. You should be sure not to contaminate the chemicals by interchanging the containers.

- **Organizing the equipment.** It is important to lay out your equipment so that you can locate it easily in the dark. Most darkrooms are organized into a wet side and a dry side. The film and the equipment you need are located on the dry side, an area where no chemicals are allowed, to prevent accidental contamination of the film with spots of chemicals. On the dry side, you should have the opener, cassette of exposed film, scissors, reel, and developing tank. On the wet side, you should place the thermometer, developer, and mixed chemicals.

- **Loading the film.** With the lights in the darkroom turned off, you take the film out of its light-tight cassette, roll the film onto a developing reel, put the loaded reel into a developing tank, and put the cover firmly on the tank. You should be sure your hands, the tank, and the reel are dry before you start loading the film. You should try to handle the film by its edges as much as possible to avoid getting fingerprints on it. The film must be fed into the reel accurately; if it jumps out of the groove and touches itself, the emulsion will be damaged and some frames will be lost.

- **Developing and fixing the image.** The developing process consists of giving the film several chemical "baths" and clear-water rinses while it is in the developing tank. The first is the developing solution, followed by other chemical solutions that stop the developer's action and then "fix" the image for permanency.

You must be sure the film is developed for the exact length of time and at the particular temperature recommended by the manufacturer. If time/temperature instructions are not followed, overdeveloped or underdeveloped negatives result. Incorrectly developed negatives are more difficult to print.

When development is complete, you pour the developer out of the tank through the small opening in the cover of the tank and pour in water or stop bath. When stop bath time is up, you pour out the water stop or stop bath and pour in the fixer. Again, the cover must remain on the tank. When the fixing time is up, you can remove the cover of the tank for the remaining chemical and water rinses. The film is no longer light sensitive.

To be sure development occurs evenly, you must agitate the film and developer in the tank. For stainless steel tanks, you cap the small opening in the tank cover and turn the tank upside down and back at the rate of three inversions in 5 or 6 seconds. Plastic tanks come with an agitator rod or a thermometer that you turn at the rate of three revolutions in 5 or 6 seconds. In either case, you should agitate for 30 seconds after you first pour in developer. After that, you should agitate for 5 seconds every 30 seconds.

Agitation during the development step affects the final results, so it is important to establish a consistent development technique. Agitation during the subsequent steps is not as critical, but you must agitate periodically to ensure even processing.

When the film is fully rinsed and processing is complete, you remove the reel from the tank and carefully unwind the film from the reel. You remove excess water from both sides of the film with a sponge or squeegee before hanging it up to dry.

- **Storing negatives.** When the developed film is dry, it's a good idea to cut it into strips of 5 or 6 frames and store the strips in a negative holder. Negatives must be stored carefully; damaged negatives are essentially useless. They must be protected from scratches that produce dark lines on the final print. They should also be stored flat to ensure sharp prints. And, they should be stored in a relatively cool and dry location to prevent stains or chemical contamination.

A Note on:

Controlling Contrast

You can control negative contrast—the range of tones in the negative—by altering development time. After developing a few rolls of film, you might find that your negative contrast is unsatisfactory. If your negatives are consistently overdeveloped and too contrasty, you can try reducing the recommended development time by 25 percent. On the other hand, if they are consistently underdeveloped and too flat, you can try increasing time by 25 or 50 percent. You should consider the manufacturer's developing time as only a starting point. It may take two or three adjustments of the developing time to achieve consistently satisfactory negatives.

You manipulate development time in order to control the contrast of your negatives, which, in turn, allows you ultimately to control the contrast of the prints that you make from your negatives. You should be able to achieve consistently good negatives—and thus good prints—by fine tuning your film development procedures to suit your equipment, shooting techniques, and materials.

How to

Develop Film

💡 **Step 1:** On the wet side of the darkroom, with the lights on, prepare the chemicals you need (developer, stop bath, fixer, hypo clear, and wetting agent) by mixing them as directed by manufacturers' instructions.

💡 **Step 2:** Be sure that the temperature of the chemicals reaches 68°F by putting the bottles of mixed chemicals in a pan containing water that partially covers the bottles. Test the temperature of the developer with a thermometer, and simply add hot or cold water to the pan until you get the desired 68°F.

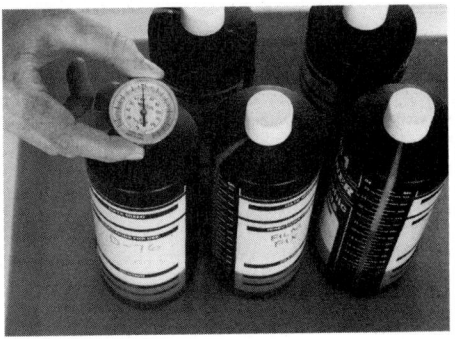

💡 **Step 3:** Organize the equipment you need so you can find them in the dark on the dry side of the darkroom. (From lower left clockwise: a can opener for the film cassette, a developing reel, a single-reel developing tank and its cover and cap, and scissors.)

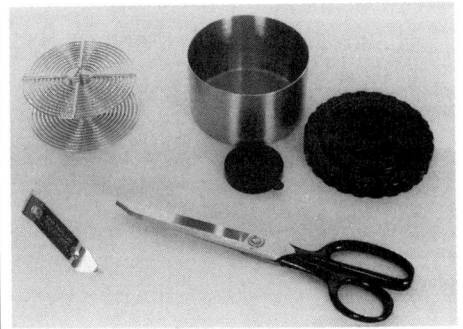

💡 **Step 3A:** If you will be developing several rolls at once in a multi-reel tank, fill the developing tank with developer almost to the top. Put the tank in the pan of water on the wet side of the darkroom. The cover should not be on the tank, but should be placed in a spot where you can locate it in the dark.

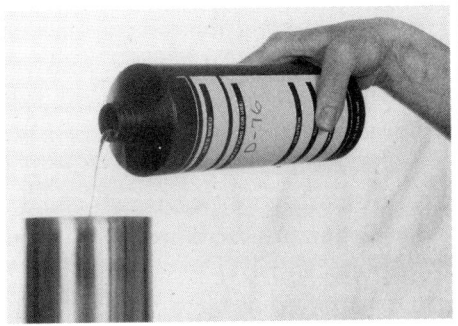

How to

Develop Film

💡 **Step 4:** Set the timer to the time indicated on the manufacturer's instruction sheet or at the time you have determined from previous development trials. At this point, however, do not start the timer.

💡 **Step 5:** Turn off the darkroom lights, and use the can opener to pry the end off the film cassette. (Note: For simplicity, these instructions deal with 35 mm film; other film sizes are covered in manufacturers' directions.) Remove the film from the cassette, and cut off a short section of the end to make it square.

💡 **Step 6:** Pick up the reel, and hold it in one hand. With the thumb and forefinger of your other hand, insert the end of the film into the clip that holds it in place in the center of the reel.

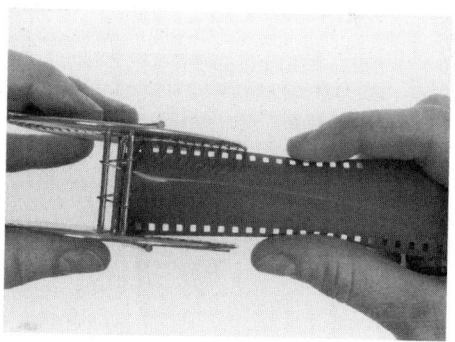

💡 **Step 7:** Pinch the film slightly between thumb and forefinger to bow it as you turn the reel with the other hand. The film should clear the outside edges of the reel and seat itself in the groove that begins at the center and spirals outward to the outside edge. You must be sure to thread the film onto the groove evenly so it does not touch itself at any point.

FOUR

How to

Develop Film

💡 **Step 8:** If you are developing only one roll, drop the loaded reel into the developing tank and put the cover firmly on the tank.

💡 **Step 8A:** If you are developing several rolls of film, place the loaded reels on the loading hook and put them in the tank filled with developer all at once. Start the timer.

💡 **Step 8B:** Step 8B: If you are using a plastic tank and reel, drop the loaded plastic reel into the plastic developing tank place the lid on the tank and then twist it to lock in place.

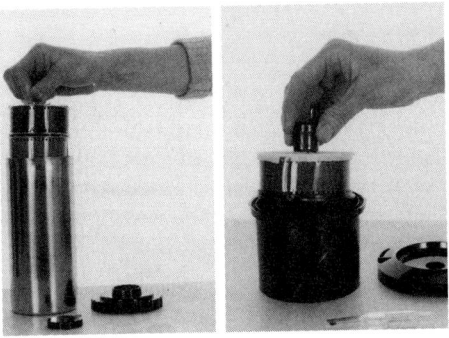

💡 **Step 9:** Pour the developer in the tank through the small opening in the cover, and then cap the opening tightly. Start the timer, and turn on the darkroom lights.

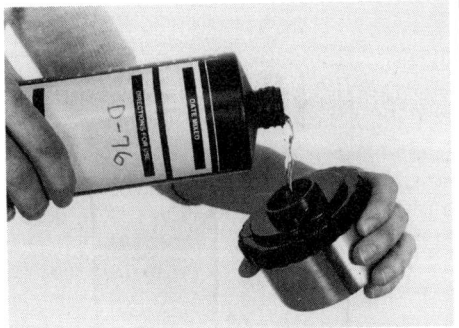

💡 **Step 10:** Rap the tank gently on the edge of the sink to dislodge air bubbles.

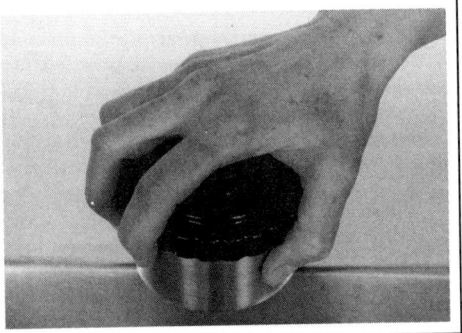

How to

Develop Film

Step 11: Pick up the tank and agitate it gently—that is, turn it upside down and back—to make sure the developer flows freely and continuously over the entire film surface. You should agitate for 30 seconds initially, then 5 seconds every 30 seconds throughout the developing time.

Step 11A : If you are developing several rolls of film, push the reels up and down to remove air bubbles. Then place the cover, with the small cap firmly in place, on the tank, and turn on the darkroom lights.

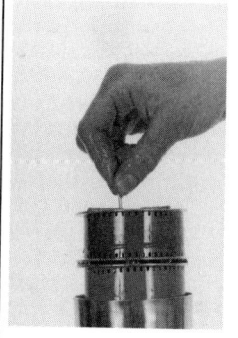
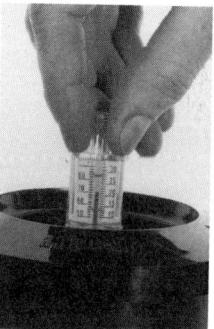

Step 11B: If you are using a plastic tank, agitate the developer by inserting the thermometer that comes with the tank and twisting it in a clockwise direction. Note that if you twist the thermometer counterclockwise, you will unwind the film.

Step 12: When the timer shows that the end of the development step is near, remove the small cap from the cover, and pour the developer out of the tank. Do not remove the tank cover. Begin pouring about 10 seconds or so prior to the end of development so all developer will be out of the tank at the end of the timing period.

Step 13: Pour stop bath or water stop into the tank through the small opening in the cover. Agitate the tank. If you are using water, change the water every 15 to 20 seconds. The cover should remain on the tank.

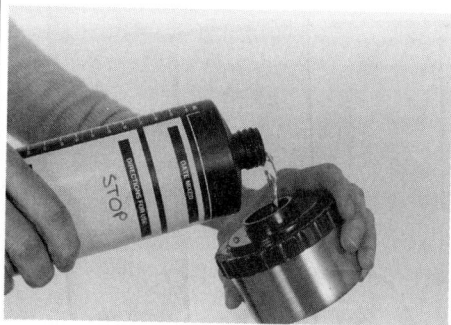

How to

Develop Film

💡 **Step 14:** At the end of the stop step, pour the stop bath back into its container, or pour out the water. Do not remove the tank cover.

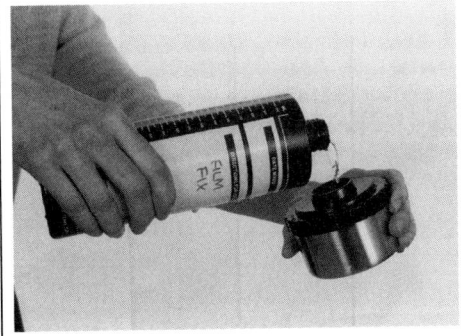

💡 **Step 15::** Fill the tank with fixer, again through the opening in the tank cover. Set the timer for 2 to 4 minutes and start it.

💡 **Step 16:** Agitate the tank, again 30 seconds initially; then 5 seconds every 30 seconds.

💡 **Step 17:** At the end of the fixing step, remove the cover, and then pour the fixer back into its container. It is now safe to take the cover off the tank since the film is no longer light sensitive.

How to

Develop Film

Step 18: Rinse off the film with running water at 68°F for approximately 30 seconds to remove excess fixer.

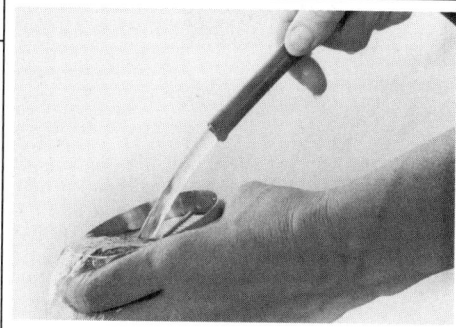

Step 19: Immerse the film in the hypo clearing agent for 1 to 2 minutes. To agitate the hypo solution, you can rock the tank gently or turn the reel in the tank periodically to swirl the solution.

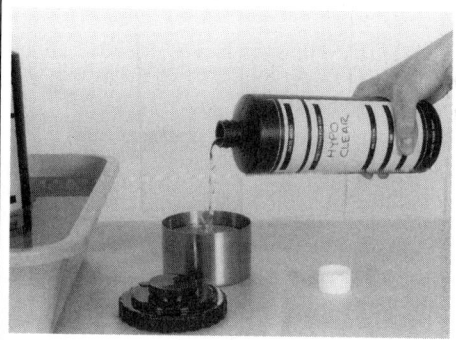

Step 20: Wash the film for 5 minutes in running water at 68°F. A specialized film washer is shown here, but you can also hold the tank under a faucet or run a hose with running water into the top of the film tank.

Step 21: Immerse the film for 30 seconds in the wetting agent. Agitation is not necessary at this step.

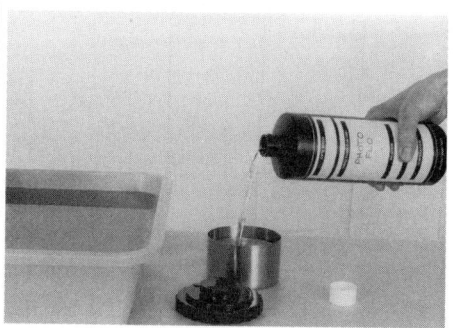

FOUR

How to

Develop Film

💡 **Step 22:** Take the reel out of the tank and carefully unroll the film. Remove excess water from both sides of the film with squeegee tongs. (Make sure the tongs are clean so the film doesn't get scratched.)

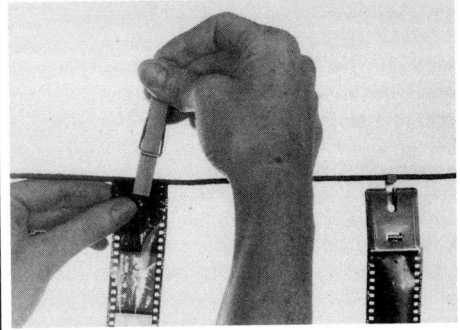

💡 **Step 23:** Hang the film to dry in a dust-free location, or place it in a film dryer if you have one. If you hang the film, weight the bottom end to take the curl out of the film.

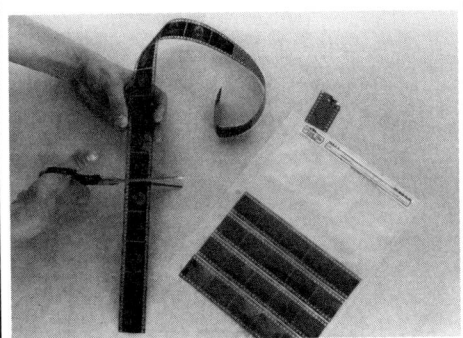

💡 **Step 24:** When the film is thoroughly dry, cut it into strips of five or six frames, depending on the negative carriers that you have acquired.

💡 **Step 25:** Store the negative strips safely in a negative sleeve.

Push Processing Film

Push processing is a widely used technique for "increasing" film speed. In fact, it does nothing of the sort, but it's a useful approximation. In simple terms, there are two steps in push processing. First, you pretend your film is more sensitive to light than it really is by inflating its speed rating when you are taking the pictures. That will consistently and precisely underexpose the film. Then, you attempt to compensate for the underexposure during development.

Push processing is most often used with films that are relatively fast to begin with—Kodak's T-Max 400 or Ilford's HP-5, for instance. These films tend to yield better results than slow or medium speed films, and if it's speed you are after, you're better off with an inherently fast film to begin with. Either of these films can be successfully pushed one or two stops.

You begin pushing film by setting your light meter with an inflated ISO speed index. To push one stop, you double the correct rating, from 400 to 800, for instance. To push two stops, you quadruple it, from 400 to 1,600. Meter readings will thus be based on a faster film than you are really using, and the film will be precisely and consistently underexposed.

If you were to develop the underexposed roll normally, you would find two deficiencies in the negatives. The frames would lack detail in the shadow areas (the dark areas of the original scene) and they would lack contrast. A print made from such negatives would be flat (lack contrast) and would show little or no detail in the dark areas. There is little that can be done about the loss of shadow detail; if it's not recorded on the film, it is difficult to salvage it later. But it is possible by push processing to build the contrast of the negative up to acceptable levels.

The push processing methods described here involve changes in the development step only. All other film processing steps—stop, fix, hypo clear, wash, and wetting agent—remain the same.

The most common method of push processing uses a special high-energy developer, quite often Acufine or Diafine. Either can be used for a two-stop push of T-Max 400, Tri-X, or HP-5 with relatively good results. There will be some loss in shadow detail, but the negatives are generally contrasty enough to be printable.

The ultimate combination for push processing, however, is T-Max developer coupled with one of the new super-fast films—Kodak's T-Max p3200 film or Fugi's Neopan 1600 Professional film. The ISO index of T-Max p3200 film is about 1000, but, as its name suggests, it is intended to be pushed to an E.I. of 3200 or higher. Fugi's Neopan 1600 is likewise intended to be pushed to an E.I. of 1600 or above. Very acceptable results can be found even when pushing these films as high as 6400 or 12,800. Best results will be obtained by using a push process developer especially suited to T-Max films, like Kodak's T-Max developer or one of the similar developers from other manufacturers.

Some photographers search as diligently for the perfect "hot soup"—the perfect push process developer—as the knights of old searched for the Holy Grail. But pushing is inherently a compromise. Push processing methods almost always entail some loss in quality—an increase in grain and a loss of shadow detail. This is the cost of getting the picture.

What Can Go Wrong

Even when you have the best of intention, things can go wrong when you are developing film. When they do, you shouldn't fret and worry. You can learn from the things that go wrong.

Problem 1 (A and B): Pinholes on negative

Pinholes (small clear spots) on the negative.

Probable Cause:

Air bubbles clung to the film during development.

Solution:

Be sure to rap the tank at the beginning of development to dislodge air bubbles.

A. Negative   B. Positive proof

Problem 2 (A and B): Negatives with glitches

Glitches or undeveloped areas on the negative.

Probable Cause:

You may have improperly loaded film onto the reel so that it touched itself in places and the developer couldn't reach the emulsion.

Solution:

Be more careful next time. In the light, practice loading an already-developed film onto a reel until you are confident.

A. Negative

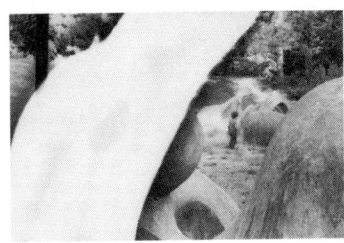

B. Positive proof

What Can
Go Wrong

Problem 3 (A):
Overexposure

Overexposure that causes negative to be too dense (too black) and contain blocked-up highlight detail.

Probable Cause:

You may have set the ISO index too low on your light meter.

Solution (B):

Make sure that you set the ISO index correctly for the film you are using. If the problem persists, check your meter against another meter.

A. Problem negative   B. Correct negative

Problem 4 (A):
Underexposure

Underexposure that results in lack of contrast and shadow detail.

Probable Cause:

You may have set the ISO index too high on your light meter.

Solution (B):

Make sure you set the ISO index correctly. If the problem persists, check your meter against another meter.

A. Problem negative   B. Correct negative

FOUR

What Can
Go Wrong

Problem 5 (A and B):
Ragged-edged areas
on negative

Probable Cause:

Your negatives may not have been fully dry when you inserted them into the envelopes or sleeves, and the sleeve stuck to the emulsion, pulling it off the film base; or, in drying, the film touched another negative.

Solution:

Make certain your negatives are absolutely dry before you put them into the envelope.

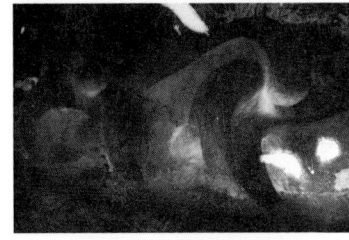

A. Negative

B. Positive proof

Problem 6 (A and B):
Scratches on negative

Probable Cause:

Fingernails or abrasive material like dust or dirt have rubbed against the emulsion; sometimes abrasive material on the camera rollers can cause scratches when loading the film.

Solution:

Handle the film very carefully, particularly while it is wet and the emulsion is soft; keep your camera free of dust and dirt.

A. Negative   B. Positive proof

FOUR

What Can
Go Wrong

Problem 7 (A and B):
Fibers imbedded in film

Fibers that become imbedded in the emulsion of the film.

Probable Cause:

You tried to dry your negatives with a paper towel, or you hung them in a location that was not free of dust.

Solution:

Be sure to dry your negatives in a dust-free location. Do not allow them to come in contact with anything except squeegee tongs until they are dry; let them dry on their own without the aid of a paper towel.

A. Negative   B. Positive proof

Problem 8 (A):
Overdeveloped negative:
too contrasty

Probable Cause:

Timer may be set improperly, or temperature of the developer is too high.

Solution (B):

Make sure that you set the timer correctly and that the temperature of the developer isn't too high.

A. Problem negative

B. Correct negative

What Can
Go Wrong

Problem 9 (A and B): Light crescents on negative

Probable Cause:

You pinched the film, probably when you loaded the film onto the developing reel.

Solution:

Handle the film more gently.

A. Negative   B. Positive proof

Problem 10 (A): Underdeveloped negative: No Contrast

Underdeveloped negative that lacks contrast.

Probable Cause:

Timer may be set improperly, or developer temperature is too low.

Solution (B):

Check the timer and make sure the temperature of the developer isn't too low.

A. Problem negative

B. Correct negative

Problem 11 (A and B): Streaks on negative

Probable Cause:

The film was not consistently agitated during development.

Solution:

Be sure to follow proper agitation procedures.

A. Negative

B. Positive proof

REVIEW
Questions

1. How does film record its images?

2. What is "structure" in film?

3. How does film react to light?

4. What are the characteristics of film?

5. What chemicals are needed to develop film?

6. How do developer, stop bath, and fixer work on film?

7. What is the role of hypo clearing agent and wetting agent?

8 What basic equipment for film developing should be in every well-equipped darkroom?

9. What steps are used to process film?

10. What is "negative contrast" and how can it be controlled?

CHAPTER FIVE

Printmaking

Untitled (Abstraction) by Laszlo Moholy-Nagy

Printmaking

Untitled (Abstraction) by Laszlo Moholy-Nagy
*(Gelatin Silver Print, n.d. 50 x 40 cm, Gift of George and Rita Barford, 1968.264. Courtesy of
The Art Institute of Chicago. Published with the permission of Hattula Moholy-Nagy)*

Lazslo Moholy-Nagy, a Hungarian photographer who came to the United States in 1937, experimented with images made without a camera by putting objects on photographic paper and exposing them directly to light—a kind of contact print he called "Photograms." This approach was also taken by Man Ray, who called his creations "Rayographs." Moholy-Nagy created his works using collages, montages, reflections, refractions—almost all camera-less images made by manipulating light through various devices. Portraiture, landscapes, nudes, architecture, machines, organic form, and urban street scenes were among his themes.

IT IS NOT NECESSARY to make prints of every frame on a roll of film. A great deal of paper and large sums of money have been wasted by occasional photographers who get all their film frames made into prints.

Professional photographers and serious students use an alternate approach. They select the frames to be made into enlarged prints by first looking at a contact sheet containing an unenlarged positive print of each frame on the roll of film they have shot.

A Guide to Photographic Paper

To make a positive print from a negative, the first thing you need is photographic paper. There are two basic kinds of paper: resin-coated paper and fiber-based paper. All papers are light-sensitive and, like film, have several layers (Figure 5.1). The most important layers are a gelatin supercoating, a light-sensitive emulsion containing silver halide crystals, and a paper base.

The **gelatin supercoating** protects the emulsion from scratches. Just as with film, when the **light-sensitive emulsion** is exposed to light, a few of the silver ions in the silver halide crystals are converted to metallic silver atoms to make a latent image. Processing makes the image visible and permanent. The **paper base** is the support for the other two layers.

In **resin-coated paper,** the paper base has a top coating as well as a subcoating, both of which are water-resistant plastic and thus prevent chemicals from seeping into the paper base during processing. Because the paper base does not absorb the chemicals, resin-coated papers process and wash quickly. They also require fewer chemicals than other papers. "RC paper," as it is called, is a relatively

FIVE

FIGURE 5.1. Structure of black and white photographic paper

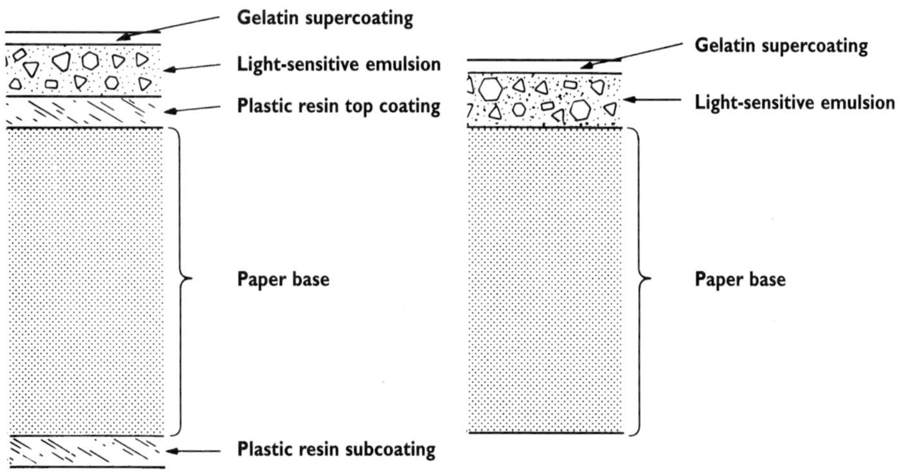

Gelatin supercoating
Light-sensitive emulsion
Plastic resin top coating
Paper base
Plastic resin subcoating

Gelatin supercoating
Light-sensitive emulsion
Paper base

A. Resin-coated photographic paper

B. Fiber-based photographic paper

FIGURE 5.2.
Various types of
photographic paper

recent innovation. Commonly used RC papers include Kodak's Polycontrast Rapid II RC, Polyfiber, and Polyprint, Ilford's Ilfospeed Multigrade, and Agfa's Brovira-Speed and Portriga-Speed.

Fiber-based paper was the only type that existed before RC papers were introduced. For many purposes, these papers are still preferred since they tend to be more permanent than the resin-coated papers. If care is taken, they can produce better looking prints. But they take more time and work to process. Because processing chemicals are absorbed into the paper, prints must be washed four or five times longer than those made on RC paper. Usually, a hypo clearing agent is used—as in film processing—to shorten the wash time. Fiber-based paper also takes longer than RC paper to dry, and special care must be taken to produce a glossy surface.

Both resin-coated and fiber-based photographic papers are manufactured by a number of companies and are boxed and packaged to be protected from light (Figure 5.2). Most papers come in various sizes and with various characteristics. The paper you decide to use will depend on the kinds of photos you take and your own preferences gained by experience in the darkroom. While you are mastering the art of printing, however, it is best to keep things as simple as possible by using resin-coated paper.

Characteristics of paper

• **Surface.** Paper surfaces vary from smooth to highly textured. A smooth surface is glossy and shiny, while the textured ones have a matte finish or dull appearance. Samples of common paper surfaces are available for inspection at nearly all photographic supply stores. Each manufacturer has its own system for classifying paper surfaces. Some use letter designations, such as "F" or "N," while others use descriptive words like "smooth" or "rough."

The choice of surface depends on the use of the photo. In photojournalism, for example, where photos are to be screened and reproduced by a printing press, they are usually printed on a glossy (F surface) paper. The glossy surface works well because it has a slightly longer tonal scale (range of tones from black to white) than other kinds of paper. Photographs to be used for other purposes are often printed on other surfaces. If a photograph is to be viewed directly, a glossy surface is usually undesirable because reflections from the shiny surface detract from the photograph itself. A matte (N surface) surface paper may be more suitable. Other surfaces (like E) offer a compromise: They produce nearly the same tonal scale as a glossy paper, but are slightly textured to reduce reflections. Ilford's "Pearl" surface is very similar to Kodak's E surface.

- **Weight.** Weight corresponds to the thickness of the paper. Fiber-based paper usually comes in single weight and double weight. RC papers, however, are medium weight. Most prints made on fiber-based paper are single weight. Double weight paper resembles the stiffness of light cardboard and is more expensive than single weight.

- **Contrast.** Most papers are also available in several contrast grades to compensate for less-than-perfect negatives. As the paper grade increases, the contrast between the black tones and the white tones increases. By adjusting film developing time, you can adjust negative contrast to yield a "perfect" print. By selecting the proper contrast grade of paper, you can adjust for slight deviations from an optimum negative.

Most papers are available in contrast grades from 0 or 4 to 5 (Table 5.1). The lower the grade number, the less contrasty is the paper, and the less contrasty is the final print (Figure 5.3).

With most papers, it is necessary to purchase separate packages of paper to get different contrasts. That is, you need to have five boxes of paper on hand to obtain contrast grades of 1, 2, 3, 4, and 5.

TABLE 5.1. Paper contrast grades

#0	Extra soft/very flat	**#3**	Hard/contrasty
#1	Soft/flat	**#4**	Extra hard/extra contrast
#2	Normal/medium	**#5**	Extreme contrast

FIVE

FIGURE 5.3. Using paper grades to control contrast

A. Contrast grade #1 paper

B. Contrast grade #3 paper

C. Contrast grade #5 paper

- **Variable-contrast papers.** Special variable-contrast papers are available that allow contrast control on the same paper through use of filters. These papers are coated with two emulsions: One is equivalent to a grade 1 paper and the other equivalent to a grade 4. The grade 1 emulsion is sensitive to yellow light. The grade 4 is sensitive to purplish light. To obtain the various grades, you use special filters that color the light coming from the enlarger. If you use a yellow filter, for example, the top emulsion layer is exposed and a contrast grade of 1 is obtained. With a purplish filter, on the other hand, the bottom layer is exposed, resulting in a contrast grade of 4. Filters of intermediate colors are used to produce intermediate contrast grades. If you don't use any filter, you'll get the equivalent of a contrast grade of 2.

Storing photographic paper

Whatever type of paper you use, it is vital that you store it carefully. Adverse storage conditions cause deterioration of both the physical and photographic properties of paper.

You should store the paper you use regularly in a cool, dry place. A temperature below 70°F is recommended, with the relative humidity between 40 and 50 percent. If you store your paper for long periods, you should put it in an area with temperatures between 40°F and 50°F and be sure to keep it away from steam pipes, radiators, or any source of heat.

You should be certain that you securely close the package or storage container for your paper. If you will be storing it for any extended period or carrying it around with you, you should tape the box so it doesn't come open accidentally. You should also be careful to keep photographic paper out of reach of curious friends who may open the packages to see what it really looks like and end up ruining it by exposure.

Chemicals and Equipment

Whether you intend to make a positive contact sheet or enlarged prints from your negatives, you need chemicals to develop and fix the image on the photographic paper. You also need certain basic pieces of equipment, as well as an enlarger.

Chemicals

You process positive prints on RC paper with chemicals similar to those used in developing film: developer, stop bath, and fixer (Figure 5.4). All three come in liquid and granular form. You should always follow manufacturers' instructions in mixing them.

- **Paper developer.** Developer brings out the image that has been projected onto the paper by the enlarger. Paper developers are generally stronger than

FIGURE 5.4.
Chemicals for making
prints: Developer, stop
bath, fixer

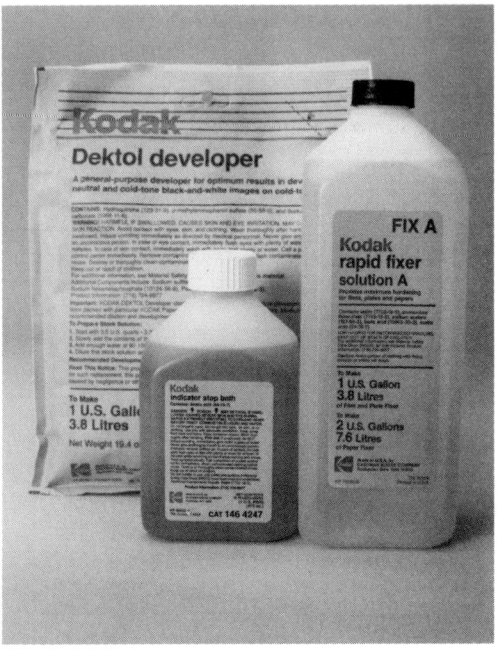

those used in film processing, and development times are correspondingly shorter. A commonly used paper developer is Dektol, which is first dissolved in water to make a stock solution. Then, to make a working solution, you mix one part of the Dektol stock solution with two parts of water. You mix up enough working solution to fill the bottom of your tray to a depth of at least 1/2".

• **Stop bath.** This solution stops the action of the developer. An acid stop bath, usually dilute acetic acid, is used in print processing.

• **Fixer.** This chemical fixes the image on the print and makes it permanent. But if you leave a print in fixer for too long, it will start bleaching it out. The same fixer can be used for both film and print processing, although fixer for printing is usually mixed to half the strength as that for fixing film. Manufacturers' instructions indicate exact amounts to use.

Basic Equipment

• **Trays** (Figure 5.5). You need one each for developer, stop bath, fixer, and wash water. Trays come in various sizes; 5" x 7", 8" x 10", or 11" x 14" are the most common. You should use a tray that is larger than the print you plan to make in order to give yourself room to work. For example, you use an 11" x 14" tray when you are working with 8" x 10" prints.

Trays for chemicals come in stainless steel, enamel, and plastic. Plastic trays are most commonly used because they are the least expensive. Plastic trays have another advantage: They come in different colors (yellow, white, black, and red, for example), and you can use the color to distinguish the type of chemicals you put into the trays without labeling them.

One tray should be set up to wash the prints. Washing can be done in a variety of ways. The simplest involves running water into a tray or bucket and letting it overflow into the sink. You may also purchase specially built wash trays that are connected to the water supply by a hose. One of the most common and efficient washing devices is Kodak's tray siphon, which attaches to a tray and siphons off the fixer-laden water as it adds fresh water.

FIVE

- **Tongs** (Figure 5.5). You use these wood, plastic, or metal devices to move prints along the line of trays in a darkroom and thus avoid putting your hands in the chemicals. Two pairs of tongs—one pair for developer and one pair for stop bath and fixer—are needed to prevent contamination of the developer with the other chemicals. Different colored tongs will help keep you from mixing them up.

- **Thermometer** (Figure 5.5). The same thermometer you use to check the temperature of the chemicals for film developing is needed for the same purpose in making prints.

FIGURE 5.5. Printmaking equipment: Colored plastic trays for chemicals, wooden tongs, thermometer, siphon wash tray, and print squeegee

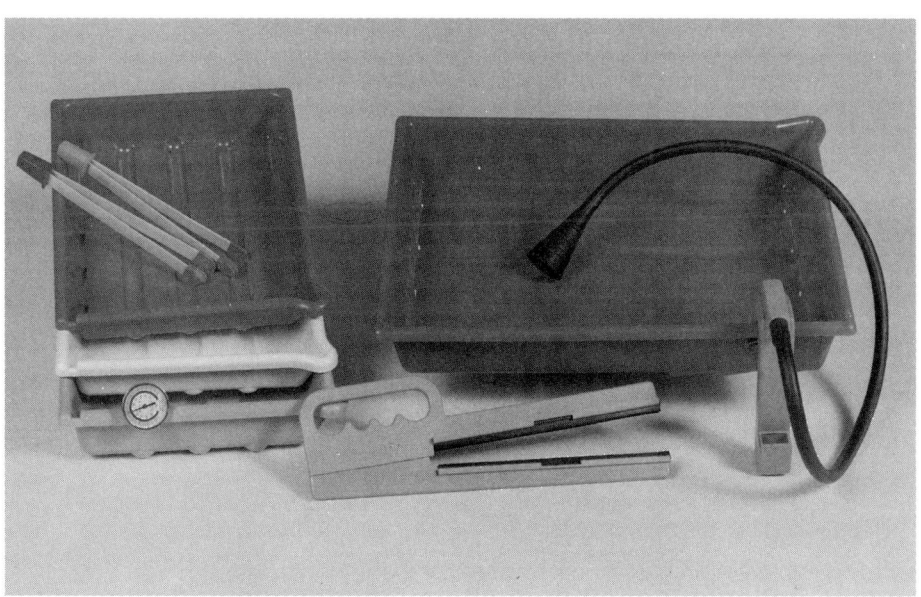

FIGURE 5.6.
Equipment for
making contact
sheets: Hinged
printing frame (left)
or plain sheet of
glass used to hold
negatives in place on
photographic paper

- **Print squeegee** (Figure 5.5). This tong—like implement has rubber on both edges. You use it to wipe excess water off your prints when you have finished rinsing them.

- **Contact printing frame** or **sheet of glass** (Figure 5.6). To hold the negatives in place on the photographic paper when you are making a contact sheet, you need a contact printing frame or a sheet of glass. If you use a sheet of glass, it must be large enough to cover an 8" x 10" sheet of paper. You can use window glass, but it breaks easily and has sharp edges. It is usually best to go to a glass shop and have a piece of plate glass cut to size and the edges beveled.

- **Timer** (Figure 5.7). It is best to use a timer with a large face that is easy to read under the dim illumination of a safelight. Specialized photographic timers are excellent, but your wristwatch or any wall clock will do. Whatever you use, though, must have a sweep second hand.

- **Dusting equipment** (Figure 5.8). You need a soft brush to remove dust and pieces of lint from your negatives and from the enlarger lens. Brushes are available in various styles and sizes. Some are anti-static to help loosen the dust and some have built-in blowers. You can also purchase pressurized cans of air that you use to blow dust away. An inexpensive alternative is an ear bulb, available at most pharmacies, which never needs to be refilled.

- **Negative carrier** (Figure 5.9). This device is used with an enlarger to hold the negative flat while the image is being projected onto the paper. The size of the carrier opening corresponds to the size of the negative.

FIVE

FIGURE 5.7. Assorted photographic timers

Figure 5.8. Dusting equipment: Pressurized canned air, ear bulb, soft brush, blower brush

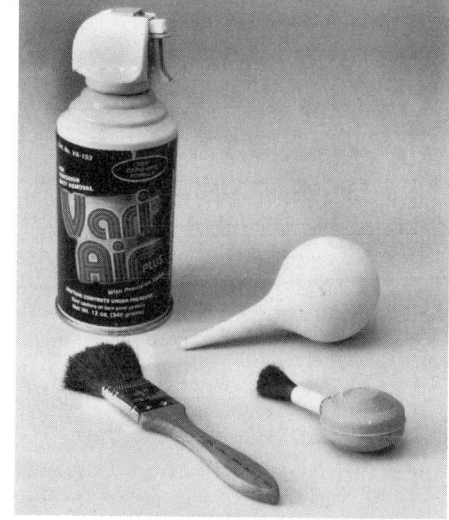

FIGURE 5.9. Metal carrier to hold negative in enlarger

A. Open carrier

B. Loaded carrier

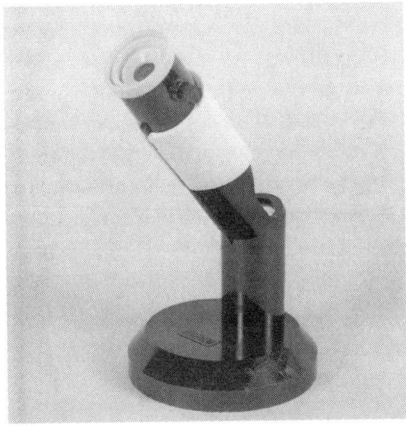

FIGURE 5.10. Grain magnifier used to check sharpness of projected negative image

FIGURE 5.11. Contrast filters used in the enlarger to control contrast of prints

•   **Grain magnifier** (Figure 5.10). This special magnifying device is used to examine the projected negative image when you are focusing the enlarger.

•   **Contrast filters** (Figure 5.11). These small sheets of colored plastic are used in the enlarger to control the contrast of the finished print, when using variable contrast paper.

•   **Safelight** (Figure 5.12). This light is specially designed to illuminate the darkroom without exposing the light-sensitive photographic paper. Your safelight must have the proper filter for the photographic paper you are using.

FIGURE 5.12.
Two styles of safelights for use in darkroom

- **Photographic paper.** You will need a supply of 8" x 10" light-sensitive paper. It is advisable to use resin-coated ("RC") paper to begin with.

The enlarger

Much depends on this important piece of equipment that enlarges negatives into prints. An **enlarger** (Figure 5.13) projects light through a negative onto light-sensitive paper to make a positive print. By adjusting the enlarger, prints can be made in various sizes. In most enlargers, the head contains a lamp with a condenser lens that concentrates light on the negative held below it in a metal carrier. The negative carrier slides onto the negative stage above the enlarging lens. The enlarger head as a whole moves up and down on a calibrated height

FIGURE 5.13. An enlarger

(Saunders/LPL Dual 35 35 mm enlarger; published with permission, The Saunders Group)

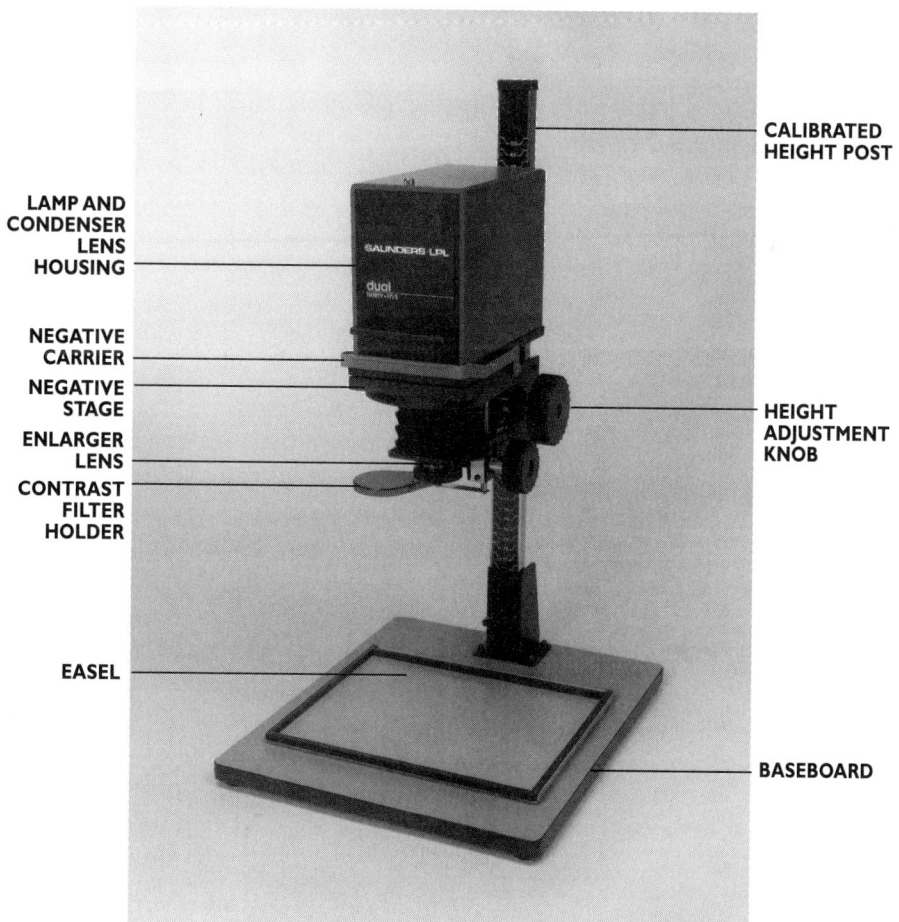

FIGURE 5.14
Adjustable and fixed easels for holding photographic paper on the enlarger baseboard

post. The movement alters the size of the image projected onto the baseboard of the enlarger. A fixed or adjustable **easel** (Figure 5.14) can be placed on the baseboard of the enlarger to hold the photographic paper in place and to mask the edges of the print to produce white borders.

Your enlarger must match the film size you use. Most enlargers can handle negatives made from 35 mm film and can enlarge each frame to about 11" x 14". Other enlargers can accommodate 2¹/₄" x 2¹/₄" roll film frames or even 4" x 5" sheet film, as well as smaller sizes.

The enlarger has exposure controls similar to those on your camera. The enlarging lens has an aperture like your camera lens. Instead of a shutter, however, it is plugged into a timer that controls the length of time the enlarger is turned on. Despite this difference, the principle is the same. You control the intensity of the exposing light with the enlarger's aperture, and you control the length of exposure with the timer. Although you can turn the enlarger lamp on and off with the switch that is attached to it, it is far more accurate to use a timer. An enlarging timer can be set to a preselected time, usually between 0 and 60 seconds. Then, whenever the "expose" button is pressed, the timer will switch on the enlarger for precisely that amount of time. Since the enlarger lacks a light meter, you do have to experiment a bit—by making a test strip—to find the correct combination of lens aperture and exposure time.

Contact Sheets: Seeing What You've Got

A **contact sheet** is a print of an entire roll of film on a single piece of photographic paper (Figure 5.15). The contact sheet allows you to see what you've got on the roll of film and to make decisions about which frames you want to enlarge. You make a contact sheet in much the same way you develop film: in the darkroom, using similar chemicals, but different equipment and techniques. In fact, now the darkroom need not be literally dark since you can use a safelight with photographic paper.

Preparing to make a contact sheet

As with film developing, you begin by mixing the chemicals according to manufacturers' instructions and checking to be sure they are at the correct temperature. You next assemble all the equipment you need. You line up the trays from left to right in the order you will use them: developer tray, stop bath tray, fixer tray, and wash tray. You should keep photographic paper on the dry side of the darkroom and in the light-tight package or in a specially built paper safe. Then you pour the appropriate chemicals in the appropriate trays and check the temperature of the chemicals and the wash water.

Your next step is to adjust the enlarger head to the height where its light projects generously over an 8" x 10" area on the baseboard. You should also

FIVE

FIGURE 5.15. A contact sheet showing all frames on film

check the enlarging lens to make sure it is free of lint and fingerprints. If not, you should carefully clean both sides of the lens with a soft brush.

If you are going to make your contact sheet on variable contrast paper, you may or may not want to use a contrast filter. If you do not use a filter, you will get the equivalent of a grade 2 paper. Whichever way you decide, you should be systematic: If you use one, use the same one all the time. That way, you can make more accurate judgments about contrast when you refer to the contact sheet. (More about contrast filters appears in Chapter 8.) By the same token, if you are using graded paper, be consistent about which contrast grade you use.

With the white lights off and the safelight on, you assemble the paper, negatives, and glass sheet into a sandwich by placing a single sheet of paper on the enlarger baseboard with its emulsion side up (that is usually the glossy side). You position the paper on the enlarger baseboard so it will be completely covered by light when the enlarger is turned on.

You next place the negatives on top of the paper, emulsion side (dull side) down. It is faster and requires less handling of the negatives if you leave the strips in their transparent sleeves to make contact prints, although the contact sheet may not be quite as sharply focused. Alternatively, you can take the negative strips out of their sleeves and arrange them individually on the paper. Either way, when the negatives are in place on the paper, you put the sheet of glass over the negatives to hold the negatives flat against the paper. At this point, before you turn on the enlarger to make your prints, it's a good idea to get in the habit of checking your package of paper to make sure you've closed it tightly.

Making a test print or a test strip

A **test print** is one that contains trial exposure times. A **test strip** is the same as a test print except only part of a piece of photo paper is used, to avoid wasting paper. You make a test print or test strip by setting the enlarger lens aperture at a reasonable f-stop and then making a series of exposures to find the time that works best with it. For contact sheets, you can begin by leaving the enlarging lens wide open (the brightest setting). Then begin the test print by making the first exposure, say, for 3 seconds, with all but a small section of the paper covered by cardboard. On the second exposure, you move the cardboard to uncover a second section of the paper and expose it, again, for 3 seconds. Meanwhile, the first section is still uncovered and is now exposed for a total of 6 seconds. On the third 3-second exposure, the first section is exposed for a total of 9 seconds, the second section for a total of 6 seconds, and the newly uncovered third section for 3 seconds. If you make a series of six 3-second exposures in this fashion, you will end up with a series of exposure times from 3 seconds (on the last section) to 18 seconds (on the first section). Then, when you have developed the test print, you can, by observation, select the correct exposure time that works with the f-stop you set to make your final prints.

To develop the exposed paper, you immerse it quickly and evenly in the tray of developer by sliding it beneath the surface. You agitate the tray gently by rocking it. Agitation prevents streaking because fresh developer swirls over the paper during development. A few seconds before the developing time is up, you pull the print from the tray to allow excess developer to drip back into the tray.

When you transfer your print from the developer to the stop bath, you should be careful not to let the tongs touch the stop bath solution in the tray. And when you remove it from the stop bath to put it into the fixer tray, you should use a second pair of tongs. You must be very careful not to contaminate the developer with either of the other two chemicals.

After the test print is totally submerged in the fixer for 10 to 15 seconds, you can look at it under white light. It is not necessary to fully process the test print, only to fix it long enough so it is stable for a few minutes under white light. You look for the section of the paper (and thus the exposure time) that gave you the best results. This section of the paper will not be so dark that detail is blocked up in the dark areas or that the whites appear dingy. On the other hand, it will not be so light that light areas are washed out and blacks are only a light gray.

If your test print is too light or too dark overall, you'll need to make another. If it is too light, it did not receive enough exposure. To correct the problem, you can increase the time of each exposure interval or open the lens aperture to a brighter setting. If it is too dark, it is overexposed. In this case, you decrease the time interval or close the lens aperture to a dimmer setting to correct the problem.

Making the contact sheet

Once you have decided on an exposure time based on the test print, you go back and repeat the process to make your contact sheet. This time, you make a single exposure of the negative-paper-glass sandwich at the selected exposure time. And you also fully fix the print according to the paper manufacturer's instructions. Lastly, you wash the print.

Now you're ready to dry the print. If you haven't a dryer suitable for RC paper, you can simply remove excess water from the print surface with squeegee tongs or a paper towel and allow it to air dry by placing it in a rack or by hanging it on a line with film clips or clothespins. Air drying RC paper takes about 15 minutes. If you want to speed it up, you can use a hair dryer. If you have an RC paper dryer, drying is accomplished in 2 to 3 minutes.

A contact sheet makes it easy to decide upon the frames you want to enlarge and print. You can use a magnifying glass for this purpose and mark the frames you like with a grease pencil. You can also make tentative **crop marks** that indicate what portion of the frame you intend to use in the final print.

Save your contact sheets along with your negatives and identify them by date and subject. You may want to print other frames at a later date.

A Note on:

Darkroom Safety

Many photographers get their hands wet when printing. They put their hands directly into the chemical tray to retrieve their prints. Normally, such contact with the chemicals doesn't cause problems. If you print a great deal, your fingernails may turn black or yellow.

Some people, however, can't touch the chemicals. They are allergic to them, usually the developer. They develop contact dermatitis, a flaming red rash, all over their hands. If that happens to you, you must get medical treatment and always wear rubber gloves when printing.

If you do handle prints directly, you must be sure to wash and dry your hands or remove the gloves before handling fresh paper or you will stain it. You can avoid such problems if you use tongs to move the print along the tray line.

It is very important for your darkroom to have good ventilation.

How to:

Make Contact Sheets

Step 1: Prepare the chemicals you need by mixing them according to the manufacturers' instructions. If your developer was mixed by using warm water, allow it to cool to about 70°F before you begin processing.

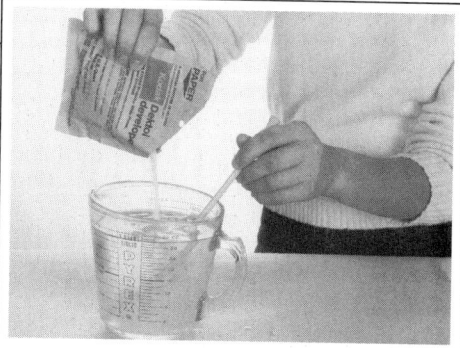

Step 2: Pour the chemicals into the appropriate trays that have been assembled close to each other in the order you will use them. Fill the trays to a depth of 1" with developer (left), stop bath (center), and fixer (right). If you plan to use a siphon wash tray, rather than the sink, for the running wash water, it should be set up next to the fixer tray.

Step 3: Check the temperature of the developer. Also check and adjust the temperature of the running wash water.

Step 4: Clean the glass you will use to hold the negatives in place on the paper.

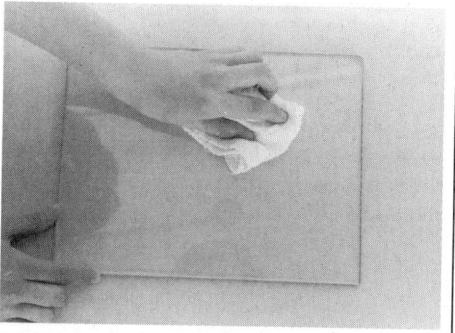

FIVE

How to:

Make Contact Sheets

Step 5: Turn off the white lights in the darkroom, and turn on the safelight and the enlarger light. Then, adjust the enlarger head so that the light projected onto the baseboard is sufficient to cover an 8" x 10" sheet of paper generously.

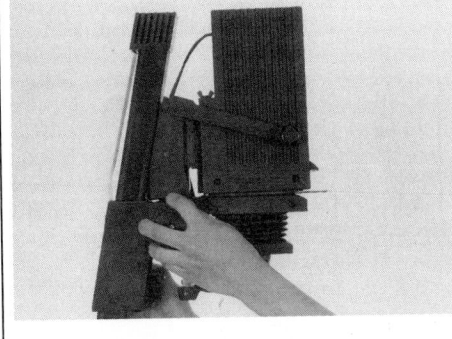

Step 6: Set the enlarging lens aperture to its brightest setting.

Step 7: Set the enlarger timer to 3 seconds, and turn off the enlarger light.

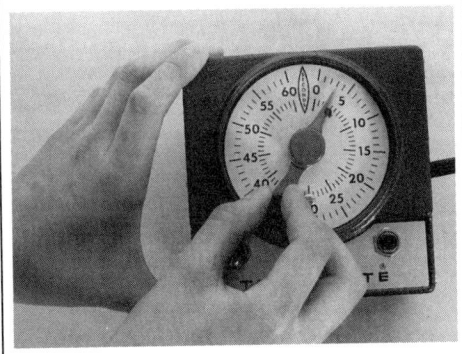

Step 8: With only the safelight on, take out a sheet of RC paper, and lay it on the baseboard of the enlarger with the emulsion side up. Position the paper so that it will be completely covered by the light projected from the enlarger when you turn it on.

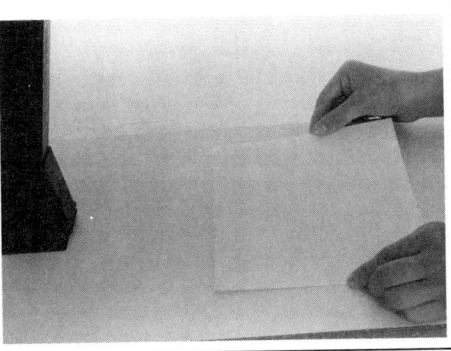

How to:

Make Contact Sheets

💡 **Step 9:** Place the sheet of negative sleeves on the paper. Or, if you prefer, arrange the individual negative strips on the paper, being careful not to touch the paper and to handle the strips only by the edges. In either case, be sure the negatives are positioned with the emulsion (dull) side down.

💡 **Step 10:** Cover the negatives and paper with the sheet of glass.

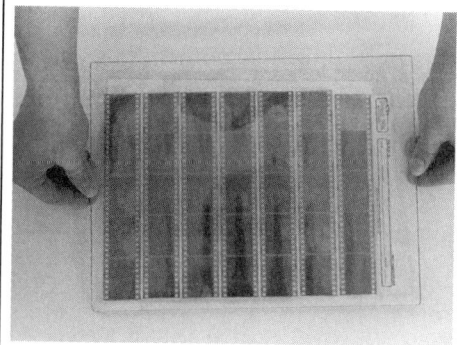

💡 **Step 11:** Begin to make a test print by using a sheet of cardboard and covering all but one row of frames on the negative strips.

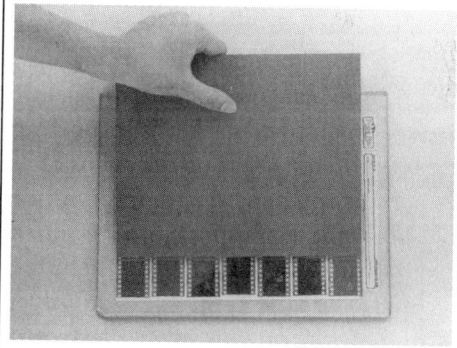

💡 **Step 12:** Press the timer button to turn on the enlarger light and expose that row of frames for 3 seconds.

How to:

Make Contact Sheets

Step 13: Move the sheet of cardboard to uncover another row of frames. Make another 3-second exposure. Continue moving the cardboard and making 3-second exposures until the entire set of negatives has been exposed.

Step 14: Handling it by the edge, remove the exposed paper from beneath the negatives.

Step 15: Set the timer or note the time on your wristwatch, and then, using tongs, slide the paper beneath the surface of the developer in the first tray.

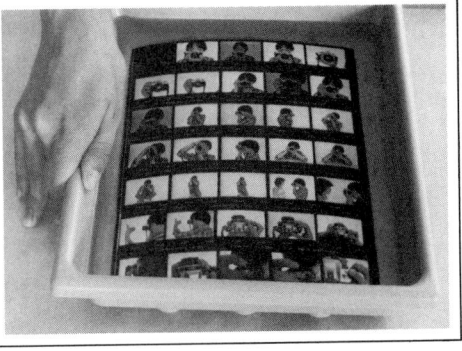

Step 16: Agitate the developer by gently rocking the tray throughout development. Leave the print in the developer for approximately 1 minute or for the amount of time specified by the paper manufacturer.

How to:

Make Contact Sheets

Step 17: About 10 seconds before the recommended time is to expire, remove the print and allow it to drip over the tray.

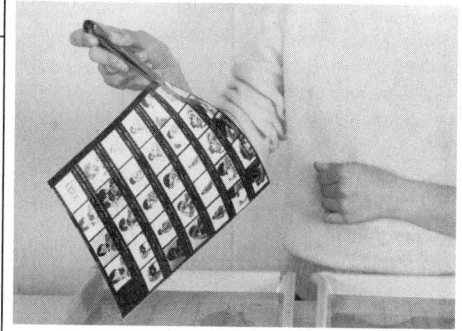

Step 18: Slide the print beneath the surface of the stop bath for 10 to 15 seconds. Then, using a second pair of tongs, remove it and let it drip over the tray.

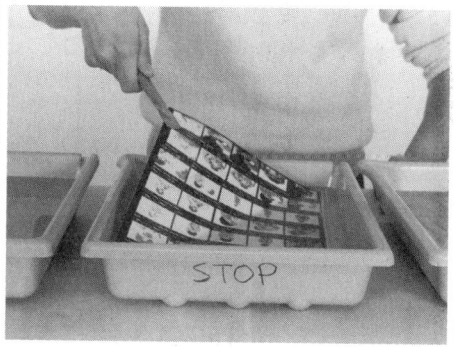

Step 19: Slide the print into the fixer for about 15 to 30 seconds (since it is only a test print).

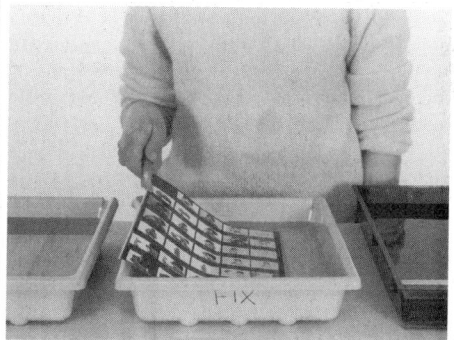

Step 20: Inspect the test print under white light to determine the correct exposure time to use, and set the enlarger's time accordingly.

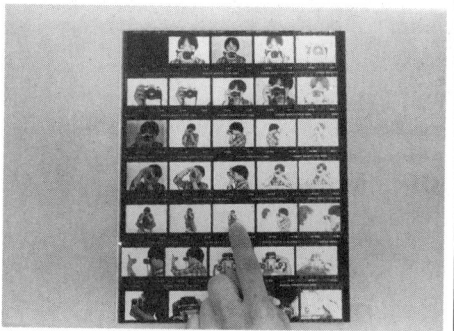

FIVE

How to:

Make Contact Sheets

💡 **Step 21:** Repeat the process of assembling paper, negatives, and glass to make a contact sheet. Then, turn on the enlarger to expose all of the negatives at one time.

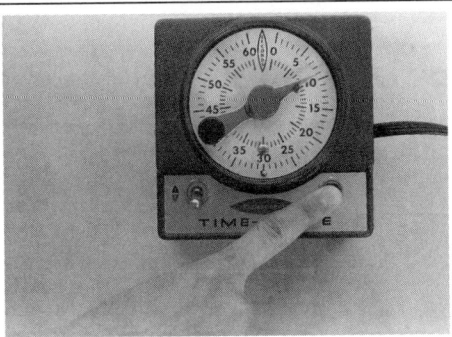

💡 **Step 22:** Develop the contact sheet as you did the test print, but extend the fixing time to a full 2 to 4 minutes, as recommended by the paper manufacturer.

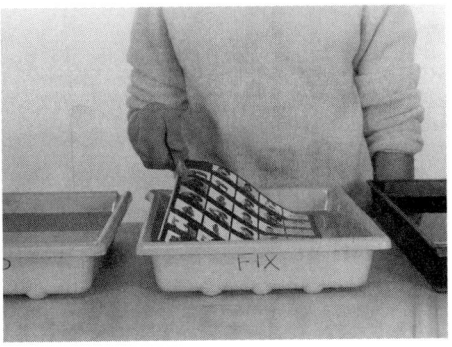

💡 **Step 23:** Wash the print for 5 minutes in running water.

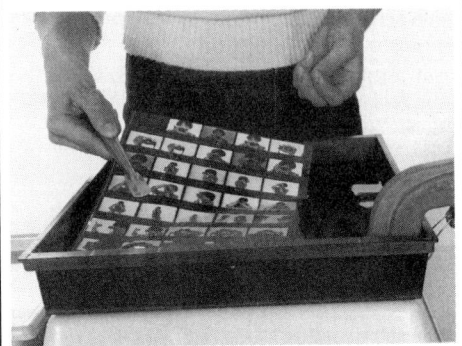

💡 **Step 24:** Use the print squeegee to mop off excess water from the print and hang it up until dry, about 15 minutes. If you have a print dryer, drying will only take a couple of minutes.

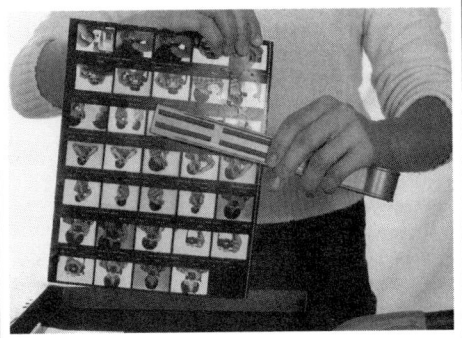

How to:

Make Contact Sheets

💡 **Step 25:** Inspect the dry contact sheet with a magnifying glass and mark frames you may want to enlarge later. Make any notes on the contact sheet you might need for later reference.

💡 **Step 26:** Store the contact sheet and negatives so they will be accessible but protected.

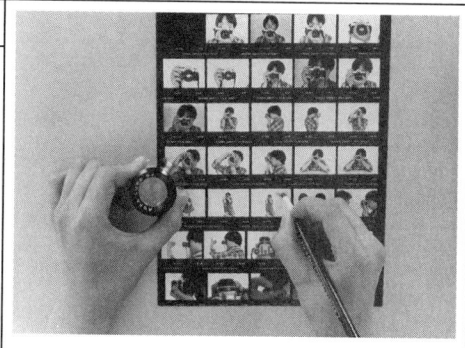

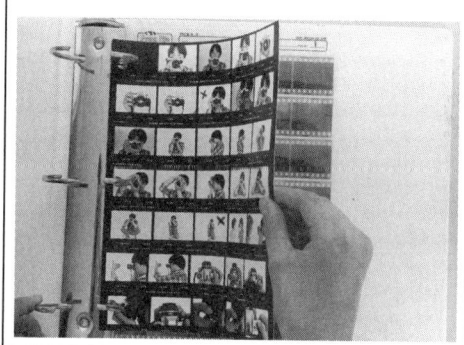

FIVE

Enlargements: Getting the Big Picture

If negatives are crucial to good photographs, the process of enlarging them goes one step beyond that in its importance. Ansel Adams has said that as the negative is the score, the print is the performance. It is when you print that you bring the picture alive.

In the darkroom, you can use the machine that does the work—the enlarger—to do some of the things you couldn't do (or neglected to do) when shooting the picture. The composition can often be improved. Extraneous elements can be eliminated. Print tonalities can be adjusted. If you have an underexposed or thin negative, you need to select a higher contrast paper and less exposure (smaller aperture and/or shorter time) or you will come out with a muddy print. If you have an overexposed or dense negative, you need to increase exposure when making the print.

Making an enlargement

The enlarging process is quite similar to the one you followed in making your contact sheets. You will need the same equipment and chemicals.

• **Preparation.** You begin by removing all the dust from the negative with a soft brush. An easy way to make sure it is clean is to hold the negative at an angle under the enlarger light. The reflecting light will reveal the dust as little sparkles. Any dust specks that are not removed will be enlarged right along with your negative and appear on your print as white blobs.

When you insert the negative into the metal negative carrier of the enlarger, you should be careful not to touch anything but the edge of the film to avoid getting fingerprints on it. The emulsion side of the negative should face down, toward the emulsion side of the paper. (The general rule, whether making contacts or enlargements, is emulsion to emulsion.)

Note that if your enlarger can be adjusted to different film formats, you must be sure to put it on the 35 mm setting at this point. You next slide the negative carrier into the enlarger and set the lens aperture wide open. By setting the lens wide open—the lowest numbered f-stop—you're provided with the brightest light to focus the projected image.

You must turn off the white lights in the darkroom and turn on the enlarger to see the negative image projected on the enlarger easel. Now you have several adjustments to make before staring to print. You can raise or lower the enlarger to change magnification. You can position the easel to capture only a portion of the negative frame and eliminate extraneous elements. With some easels, you can adjust the metal edges to the exact shape and size you want in the final print.

If you will be using a contrast filter, you should place it in the enlarger before you focus. Once you've arranged things as you want them, you focus the enlarger carefully. Various types of focusing aids are available to assist you. A grain magnifier of some type is best; they are more difficult to learn to use but are very accurate. The enlarger should always be focused with the lens aperture wide open—that is, at the brightest setting. Once focused, however, you should close the aperture to f/8 or f/11—usually the optimum aperture for an enlarging lens—before you turn off the enlarger.

• **Test print or test strip.** You make a test print or test strip for an enlargement (Figure 5.16) in much the same way as you make a test print or test strip for a contact sheet. For reasons of economy most photographers use one-fourth of a full sheet when making test prints; this is called a test strip, as already noted. Again, you want to determine the exposure time that gives the best detail in both shadows and highlights. Experience will eventually guide you in the selection of a trial exposure time for test prints. For now, you can try using an interval of 5 seconds. As with contact sheets, you begin by covering all but about 2" of the

FIGURE 5.16.
A test print showing interval exposure times in seconds

FIVE

sheet of paper with cardboard and making a single 5-second exposure. Then you move the cardboard to expose another 2" and make a second 5-second exposure. You keep moving the cardboard and making exposures until the entire paper has been exposed.

You process the exposed paper for an enlargement just as you did the contact sheet: Develop for 1 minute (or time recommended by paper manufacturer), stop for 15 to 20 seconds, and fix for about 30 seconds. As before, this fixing time isn't long enough for permanence, but it will allow you to inspect the print in white light. You need to select the exposure strip that gives the best detail in both shadow and highlight areas. Before you turn off the white lights, you should set your timer for the exposure time used for that section.

• **Final print.** To make the final print, you use a fresh sheet of paper, expose it for the selected time, and process it as you did the test print. This time, however, you must extend the fixing time to a full 2 to 4 minutes for permanence and wash the print for 5 minutes before drying it.

You now have what photographers call a "straight" print—one that hasn't been manipulated at all. Usually, it's only the beginning. It is a rare print that can't be improved with some extra work. We will look at how to improve your prints in the next chapter.

How to:

Make Enlargements

Step 1: Pour the prepared chemicals into assembled frays as you did to make contact sheets.

Step 2: Check the temperature of the developer and running wash wafer. They should both be close to 68°F.

Step 3: Use a soft, anti-static brush to clean the enlarger lens.

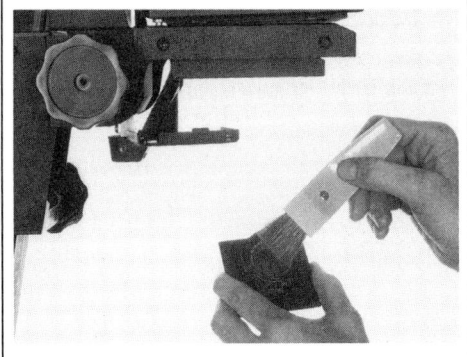

Step 4: Clean the negative you plan to print using a soft brush. Be sure all dust specks are removed.

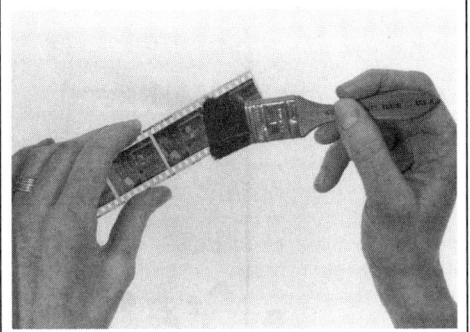

FIVE

How to:

Make Enlargements

💡 **Step 5:** Insert the negative strip into the negative carrier, being careful not to touch anything but the edge. Position the strip so that the frame you want to enlarge is centered in the opening of the carrier.

💡 **Step 6:** Place the carrier containing the negative strip in the enlarger head on the negative stage.

💡 **Step 7:** Set the enlarging lens aperture wide open (brightest setting). Then, turn off the white lights and turn on the safelight.

💡 **Step 8:** Turn on the enlarger to project the negative image on the enlarger easel. Then, adjust the enlarger head, as well as the easel, so the negative will be enlarged and cropped as you want it.

How to:

Make Enlargements

Step 9: If you intend to use a contrast filter, insert it in the filter holder of the enlarger.

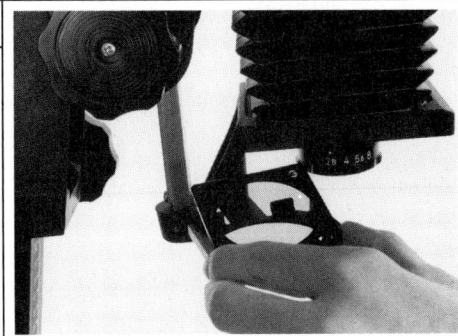

Step 10: Focus the enlarger by turning the focusing knob. You can use a grain magnifier, if you have one, to check the sharpness of the image projected on the easel.

Step 11: Set the enlarger aperture to either f/8 or f/11.

Step 12: Set the enlarger's timer to a trial time interval: for example, 5 seconds. Experience will guide you in choosing a reasonable time for the degree of enlargement and density of the negative you are using.

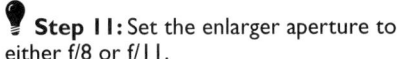

How to:

Make Enlargements

💡 **Step 13:** Turn off the enlarger, and put a sheet of PC photographic paper in the easel.

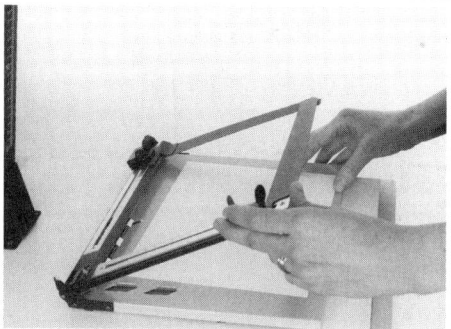

💡 **Step 14:** Using a sheet of cardboard as you did with the contact sheet, make a test print by giving several exposures to the paper.

💡 **Step 15:** Process the test print just as you did the test print for the contact sheet: Develop for 1 minute, stop for 10 to 15 seconds, and fix for 15 to 30 seconds.

💡 **Step 16:** Inspect the test print to determine the best exposure time, and set the enlarger's timer to that time.

FIVE

How to:

Make Enlargements

Step 17: With only the safelight on in the darkroom, place a fresh sheet of paper in the easel, and turn on the enlarger to expose it.

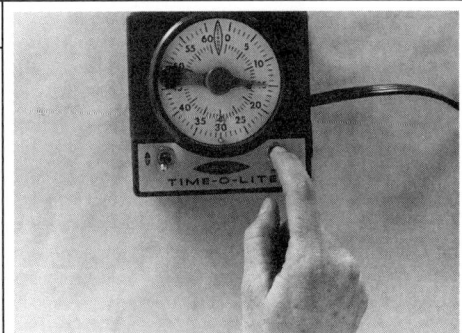

Step 18: Process the print in developer for 1 minute or so and in the stop bath for 10 to 15 seconds.

Step 19: Fix the print for a full 2 to 4 minutes, and wash in running water for a full 5 minutes.

Step 20: Remove excess water from the print with the print squeegee, and dry the print by hanging it up or by putting it in an RC paper dryer.

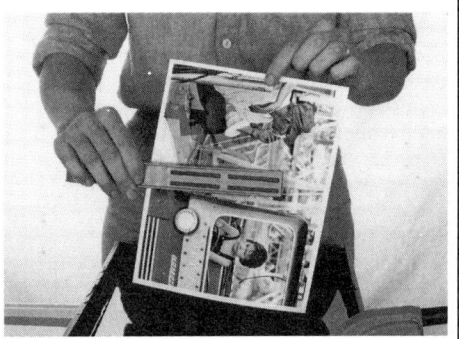

What Can
Go Wrong

Gradually, your work in making prints will come naturally. You will be able to follow all of the procedures without difficulty. At first, however, you may run into some of these common problems.

Problem 1 (A):
Overly contrasty print

Contrasty print with blacks where there should be shadow detail and whites where there should be highlight detail.

Probable Cause:

You selected the wrong filter or paper grade.

Solution (B):

Use a lower contrast filter in the enlarger or select a lower grade of paper.

A. Problem Print   B. Solution Print

Problem 2: Yellow stains on print

Yellow stains on print, frequently appearing several days or several weeks after the print was made.

Probable Cause:

You did not fix long enough or you used fixer that was weak and exhausted. This problem can also be caused by contaminated developer or insufficient washing.

Solution:

Do not use old chemicals, and be sure to wash and fix your prints sufficiently.

FIVE

What Can
Go Wrong

Problem 3: Fuzzy print

Fuzzy, out-of-focus print.

Probable Cause:

You may not have properly focused the enlarger, or your negative may not be sharp.

Solution:

Use a grain magnifier to check the projected negative image for sharpness. When your enlarger is not in focus, the grain of the negative will not be sharp. If the grain is sharp but the image is fuzzy, the negative is not sharp, and you cannot correct the problem in printing.

Problem 4:
Dark print

Probable Cause:

Print is overexposed, either because the exposure time is too long or because the enlarger lens aperture is too large.

Solution:

Decrease your enlarger exposure time, or decrease the aperture opening.

Problem 5:
Light print

Probable Cause:

Print is underexposed, either because the exposure time is too short or because the enlarger lens aperture is too small.

Solution:

Increase your enlarger exposure time, or increase the aperture opening.

What Can
Go Wrong

Problem 6:
Streaked print

Uneven or streaked print.

Probable Cause:

You did not agitate the print sufficiently in the developer.

Solution:

Rock the tray gently, but constantly, as the print is developing.

Problem 7 (A): Flat print

No contrast between dark and light tones.

Probable Cause:

You may not have developed your print for the recommended length of time; short development times don't allow sufficient blacks to build up on the paper.

Solution (B):

Develop your print for the recommended amount of time; if that isn't the problem, use a higher contrast filter in the enlarger.

A. Problem Print

B. Solution Print

REVIEW
Questions

1. What are the two basic kinds of paper?

2. What are the characteristics of photographic paper?

3. How should photographic paper be stored?

4. What chemicals are needed in making prints?

5. What basic equipment is needed in making prints?

6. What does an enlarger do and why is it important in making prints?

7. What is a contact sheet and why is it important in printmaking?

8. How do you make a test print?

9. How do you make a contact sheet?

10. How should photographers care for their hands to avoid harm from chemicals?

CHAPTER SIX

MORE ABOUT
Printmaking

"Optic Parable (Parabola Optica)" by Manuel Alvarez-Bravo, 1931

MORE ABOUT
Printmaking

"Optic Parable (Parabola Optica)" by Manuel Alvarez-Bravo, 1931
*(Gelatin Silver Print 23.5 x 17.8 cm, The Museum of Modern Art, New York. Gift of June Sidman.
Copy Print. ©1997 The Museum of Modern Art, New York)*

In a career that has extended over seven decades, Manuel Alvarez Bravo has become Mexico's greatest photographer. In 1996, at 94, he was still working in his studio in the Coyoacan district of Mexico City. "I don't go out to take photographs with a plan," he told art critic David Lyon in a 1990 interview. "I take the pictures with my eye, not my mind."

The photographer is very selective in what he decides to print from the many frames he takes. "He is ruthless in culling the good from the almost-good images," writes Lyon, "more ruthless yet in choosing those to print as part of his body of collected work."

This photo illustrates that point well. At first glance, the casual viewer is not certain what is being seen. A closer look reveals something interesting and unique: eyes and glasses and signs—all in reverse and in the reflection of an optician's shop window. The image is a kind of paradox—precisely what Manuel Alvarez Bravo probably intended all along.

BEYOND THE MECHANICS of making a straight print are the specialized darkroom techniques essential to making an effective print. For the most part, these techniques offer ways of dealing with problem negatives. In a more positive sense, however, they offer ways of interpreting the image on the negative.

As you print, you should consider what it is you want the print to convey. What is essential to the print? What can safely be eliminated? What should be emphasized? And what subdued? A photographic print is an act of communication. In the darkroom, you can make your prints speak as eloquently as possible.

Controlling Contrast in Printing

A crucial characteristic of a good print is its contrast. A print with **proper contrast** contains a solid black, a bright white, and the full range of tones between. A print lacking contrast is said to be muddy or flat. A **flat print** contains dark gray instead of blacks and light grays instead of white. A print with too much contrast is said to be hard or contrasty. A **contrasty print** contains solid blacks and whites, but at the expense of shadow or highlight detail. Shadows are blocked up to a solid black and show no details. Highlights are bleached out and lack detail.

SIX

The best way to control contrast is to adjust **film development time.** If your negatives are consistently too flat, you can increase your developing time. If they are consistently too contrasty, you can decrease the developing time. But even if you use a proper developing time, some frames on the film may still be too flat or too contrasty, and you will have to try and correct them in printing.

Contrast filters

Contrast filters and variable-contrast paper can be used to correct contrast in a print. Contrast filters are usually numbered 1, $1^1/_2$, 2, $2^1/_2$, 3, $3^1/_2$, and 4. The whole numbers (1, 2, 3, 4) correspond to grades of paper. Thus, with variable-contrast paper and contrast filters, you can make prints in between paper grade contrasts.

As in paper grades, the contrast filter numbers range from least contrasty (#1) to the most contrasty (#4). As you go from a #1 filter to a #4 filter, the whites get whiter and the blacks get blacker. Using a higher numbered filter with variable-contrast paper usually requires more exposure. Additional exposure is achieved by increasing time or by using a larger aperture, or a combination of both.

If a contrast filter is not used, variable-contrast paper reacts as if a #2 filter had been used. You can obtain a more limited range of tones on the print by using a lower numbered contrast filter (#1 or #$1^1/_2$). Conversely, you can achieve a greater range of tones by using the highest numbered contrast filter (#4). To give the print only slightly more sparkle or contrast, you use a #3 filter.

If the negative itself is too contrasty, you can try using one of the lower filters

(#1 or #1¹⁄₂) to compensate and achieve a normal print. If the negative is flat, a #3¹⁄₂ or #4 filter will improve the contrast in the print. (If you are using graded papers, you can achieve the same result by changing paper grades.) Inspecting a test print or contact sheet helps you select the proper filter or the proper grade of paper to use for your final print.

Cropping Your Prints

Cropping is nothing more than selecting a portion of the negative frame to appear in the finished print (Figure 6.1). You make cropping decisions when first shooting the photograph. You decide how to frame the photograph: where to stand, how close to get to the subject, what to include, and what to exclude from the frame. Cropping at the enlarger allows you to refine that frame.

L-shaped guides can help you visualize how a certain crop will look. You can make two **L-shaped croppers** out of cardboard and hold them together to form

FIGURE 6.1.
An example
of cropping

A. Full frame print

B. Cropped print

FIGURE 6.2.
L-shaped croppers

an adjustable "picture frame." You can put the croppers over various parts of a test print to see how different crops look before actually cropping at the enlarger. If you make small guides, you can do much the same thing directly on the contact sheet (Figure 6.2). Then, when you are working at the enlarger, you adjust the magnification and the easel to match your crop.

Cropping techniques

• **Improve your composition by cropping to change the placement of the subject.** You can decide more precisely where to place the subject in order to develop a focal point in the composition. You can also make the photo more interesting by moving the subject out of the center and placing it according to the "rule of thirds" discussed in Chapter 3.

• **Make your photographs more dramatic by cropping them to emphasize patterns and lines.** For example, you can turn a dull square photo into a more interesting horizontal or vertical one by following the patterns and lines of the subject in the photo. You can also crop to "straighten out" a tilted horizon or a leaning telephone pole.

• **Make your photographs more meaningful by cropping as tightly as possible.** Basically, that means you should eliminate anything in the photograph that isn't the subject or doesn't contribute to the subject. In this way, you can make the meaning of your picture clearer.

• **Salvage a scratched or damaged negative by cropping out such areas.** Sometimes, you can take advantage of a scratch to crop more tightly. For example, a photo of a face can often turn out more interesting if you have to crop out the back or top of the head in order to eliminate a blemish in the negative.

It's a good rule to crop tightly, but it can't be applied mechanically. You must be careful not to sacrifice the meaning of the photograph. For instance, a photograph intended to depict the "aloneness" of a subject probably can't be cropped close to the subject. If it were, a viewer couldn't tell the subject was alone. Such a photograph is likely to be stronger if a large expanse of emptiness surrounds the subject. To crop effectively when shooting the picture and when making the enlargement, you must first know what meaning you want to convey.

Manipulating Lights and Darks in Printing

If parts of your enlargement are too light or too dark, you can make adjustments in the print by **dodging** and **burning** (Figures 6.3 and 6.4). These two darkroom techniques allow you to give different exposures to different parts of a print. They are not special techniques; nearly every print you make will require some dodging and burning.

Dodging and burning techniques

Dodging entails covering a dark area during the exposure to limit the amount of light it receives relative to the rest of the print. Dodging is best accomplished with a dodging tool—a piece of cardboard attached to the end of a wire (Figure 6.5). You can also use your hand, one finger, or a small piece of cardboard.

• To dodge a print, you simply shade the portion of the print you want to lighten during part of the exposure time. The longer you shade the area, the lighter it will be. In order to blend the lightened area in with the rest of the

A Note on:

The Limitations of Cropping

One limitation on cropping is the degree you can magnify the negative. If you crop a small portion out of the negative and then magnify it a great deal to make a normal size print, you will lose print quality. The grain in the negative will be more obvious. Any slight unsharpness in the picture will be increased. In general, the more of the original frame you can use, the better the print will be, at least technically. It's an old photographic truism that if you wanted it cropped that tightly, you should have taken it that way in the first place. Cropping at the enlarger should be a matter of refinement, not wholesale revision.

FIGURE 6.3. Manipulating a print by dodging

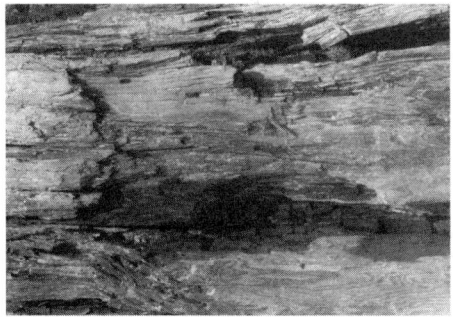

A. Unmanipulated print

B. Dodged print

A. Unmanipulated print

B. Burned print

**FIGURE 6.4.
Manipulating a print
by burning**

FIGURE 6.5. Dodging tool   **FIGURE 6.6. Burning tool**

print, you hold the dodging tool or your hand several inches above the easel and keep it moving slightly during the exposure.

• Burning involves giving more exposure time to a light area to burn in the details while protecting other areas from receiving too much exposure. Burning in large areas like a sky is best done with a piece of cardboard (Figure 6.6). For burning in smaller areas, you can cut a hole in the cardboard. You can also use your hands by cupping or spreading them to keep enlarger light away from all areas on the paper except where the picture is too light. Again, you need to keep the cardboard or your hand above the paper and keep moving it in order to blend the burned area into the rest of the print.

Dodging and burning techniques make printmaking a two-stage exposure process. The first stage is the "base" exposure—that is, the exposure for the time you selected from the test print. The base exposure creates the overall image on the paper. During the base exposure, you do any dodging needed to lighten the dark areas of the print. The second stage consists of giving areas of the print additional exposure time needed to burn in and darken them. Experience improves dodging and burning. Practice will help you get a feel for how long to dodge or burn to achieve a certain print density.

- **Timing**. You may find it helpful to think about dodging and burning in terms of exposure stops. In this case, one stop is equivalent to opening or closing the enlarger aperture lens one stop or changing the exposure time by half or double. If you burn in an area for a second "base" exposure, you will have increased exposure in that area by one stop. If you dodge for half the "base" exposure, you will decrease exposure in the dodged area by one stop.

For example, if your base exposure is 20 seconds and you dodge a certain area for 10 seconds out of the 20, you will have given the dodged area one stop less than the rest of the print. If you burn in another area for a second full 20-second exposure (40 seconds total), you will have given it one stop more exposure.

In order to increase the exposure in the burned area by two stops, you must double the total exposure again. Thus, it would be necessary to burn it in three times in addition to the base exposure—that is, to increase burning time to 60 seconds and total exposure time for the burned area to 80 seconds. On the other hand, to cut the exposure in a dodged area a full two stops, you would increase the dodging time by half—from 10 seconds to 15 seconds. You should note that dodging affects print density more quickly than burning.

Inspecting a test print will help you to visualize what difference a one stop exposure increase or decrease makes. Keep in mind that it is difficult to see exposure differences of less than about $1/3$ stop. Thus, if your base exposure were 15 seconds, burning for less than about 5 seconds would have a negligible effect. At the same time, dodging for less than about $2^1/2$ seconds would hardly be noticeable.

Bleaching darks in your prints

Occasionally areas of a print need to be lightened, but dodging would be too complicated or awkward. This can happen if too many areas need to be dodged

A Note on:

Dodging and Burning

A viewer's eye tends to be drawn to the brighter areas of a print. As a result, photographers commonly burn down the edges and corners of a print very slightly to focus attention more on the center, where the subject is likely to be. This isn't a rule, so you shouldn't feel bound by it. But it does point up how dodging and burning can be used as interpretive techniques, to control emphasis in a print. But they should be employed subtly. Prints that are obviously manipulated generally have an artificial, mechanical look to them. Instead of strengthening the image, heavy-handed manipulation distracts from it.

FIGURE 6.7. Lightening dark areas by bleaching

A. Unbleached print   B. Bleached print

at once or if the areas to be dodged are too intricate. Dodging is a way of rough hewing the print; bleaching the print gives you more precision.

Bleaching is the process of chemically lightening—or even removing—dark areas on a print (Figure 6.7). Special products are available for bleaching (Figure 6.8). "Spot Off" is a convenient, already prepared set of two chemicals, an accelerator and a bleacher. Farmer's reducer, an old photographic recipe, is available in packets. But a dilute solution of potassium ferricyanide works about as well as anything else. A pinch of the ferricyanide crystals added to water makes a light yellow bleach. A more dilute solution bleaches more slowly; a stronger solution, more quickly.

All of the bleach products work by converting the metallic silver that forms the photographic image back into silver halide salts. You then remove the silver salts by fixing again.

• **Bleaching technique.** Done well, bleaching is a slow and rather painstaking process requiring a lot of patience. It's a good idea to practice bleaching on a waste print first to help get the feel, especially if you haven't done it before.

You begin by wetting the print in a tray of fixer. Then you blow the excess fixer away from the area you plan to bleach and apply the bleach carefully to that area. If it's a large area, you can use a cotton swab. For very small areas, you can use a small watercolor brush. After about 20 seconds, you place the print back in the fixer for 15 seconds or so. You can rub your finger or the print tongs very gently over the bleached area to remove the yellow stain. If necessary, you repeat the process to lighten the area even more. It helps to keep a second print handy for reference to see how things are progressing. After you have bleached the area as intended, you must fully fix and wash the print again.

Correcting Spots on Your Prints

Perhaps Lady Macbeth said it best: "Out, damn spot. Out, I say." No matter how carefully you clean the dust off your negatives. No matter how clean you keep your darkroom (more about that later). No matter how carefully you handle your negatives. No matter that you follow all the directions in the book. You will still—sometimes—get spots on your prints.

White spots

The tiniest piece of dust, sitting quietly on your negative in the enlarger, is magnified along with the negative and becomes an unsightly white blemish. Don't despair. You can remove it via a process called, logically enough, spotting.

Spotting involves adding dye to the print until the tone of the spotted area corresponds to the tone of the part of the print adjacent to it. You use a small, pointed brush and liquid photographic dye, called Spotone (Figure 6.9). The dye comes in several different colors, and you need to mix it to get the color that matches the tone of the print to be spotted. The directions that come with the dye give the proportions to use for the paper you are using. A number 0000 watercolor brush works well for applying the dye.

• **Spotting technique.** Once you've mixed the dye to obtain the correct tone, you'll need to dilute a small amount to match the shade of gray that surrounds

FIGURE 6.8. Products for bleaching prints

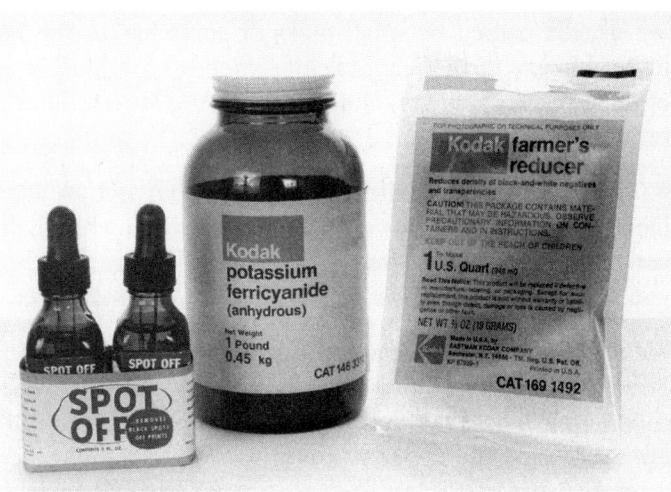

FIGURE 6.9.
Repairing—or "spotting"—white spots on a print

the spot. It's best to mix a drop of the dye with a few drops of water and test it on a scrap print. The dye should be just a bit lighter than the area you will spot. It is very important to get the excess dye off the brush and to work with an almost dry brush on a dry print. You start from the center of the spot and work outward, stippling the dye into the white spot. You must work carefully so that the dye does not overlap tones around the spot.

Spotting, like bleaching, is a painstaking process. Unlike bleaching, however, if something goes wrong, you can usually just rewash the print to remove the dye and start over.

Black spots

Very occasionally, you will encounter a black spot on your print. Black spots are usually caused by small nicks or scratches in the negative. They almost invariably end up in the middle of someone's forehead or as a blob in an expanse of open sky, looking very much like a flying saucer. They are always difficult to remove.

• **Bleaching.** Often the best solution, but not an attractive prospect, is to bleach out the spot. However, that will leave a white halo on the print, which you must then spot in to match the surrounding area. By the time you are finished, you'll feel much more like a painter than a photographer.

• **Reprinting techniques.** Reprinting can eliminate or subdue the spot. Sometimes you can reprint the photograph and take some steps to eliminate or subdue the spot. Frequently, a small scratch in the negative can be hidden by evenly coating the negative frame with an oily substance. The oil fills in the scratched area so it is less likely to refract light and cause a dark scratch mark on the print. You can buy commercial products for this purpose. An old standby is Edwal No-Scratch.

But you can often get by with what photographers inelegantly refer to as "nose grease." Most of us spent our early teen years worrying about oily skin. Now you can use it to advantage: Smear a bit of skin oil from beside your nose over the entire surface of the negative frame. (If you wear makeup, you can use skin oil from behind your ear.) When you make the print, you will usually find the scratch mark has disappeared or, at least, isn't as apparent. When you finish printing, you must be sure to clean the oil from the negative with negative cleaner.

Not to rub it in, of course, but the best solution would have been to store the negatives carefully in the first place so they didn't get scratched.

Mounting Your Prints

You can preserve your prints and best display them by mounting them onto cardboard. **Dry mounting** the print onto special mounting board by heating the print, adhesive, and cardboard under pressure is the best way to preserve prints permanently. For this process, you need drymount tissue, a paper cover sheet, mounting board, a cutter (a metal straightedge and mat knife work well), a tacking iron, and a heated mounting press.

The dry mount tissue is coated with adhesive that melts and forms a bond when it is heated. When heated under pressure, the adhesive penetrates the fibers of the board and the print and bonds them together. Many photographers prefer to use acid-free mounting board; it is more expensive than other types,

SIX

A Note on:

Darkroom Cleanliness

No discussion about printmaking would be complete without a word about darkroom cleanliness. A photographer's darkroom should be immaculate at all times. You should clean the trays and sink to prevent chemical deposits from building up. If necessary, you should scrub them down with a non-abrasive cleanser periodically. Every few months you should mop down all walls and ceiling with a damp sponge to remove collected dust. If you can, you should blow out the enlarger periodically with compressed air to remove dust. It goes without saying (but we'll say it anyway) that there should be no chemical spills on the enlarger baseboard or adjacent counters.

Remember, dust and dirt are your mortal enemies. A darkroom should be as clean as an operating room.

but desirable where permanence is needed. Other less neutral boards may eventually cause stains on the mounted print.

Dry mounting techniques

Before you begin, you must make sure everything is free of dust and dirt. Dirt particles can cause permanent bumps on the mounted print. You also need to decide on a size for the mounting board. You can mount the print on a board that is several inches larger than the print and leave a border between the edge of the print and the edge of the board. The width of the border can vary according to your preference, but you generally have better visual balance if the bottom border is wider than that at the top and sides. You can also **bleed mount** the print—that is, let the photo extend to all four edges of the board, with no border. In this case, you can begin with a board that is the same size or only slightly larger than the print.

• **With a press.** You preheat the mounting press and the tacking iron to the temperature recommended by the paper manufacturer. RC papers cannot stand high temperatures, and if you do not follow the manufacturer's instructions, the plastic coating on the paper will melt and blister. After the press is heated, you preheat the mounting board in the press to remove moisture from it.

Next, with the print face down on a clean, flat surface, you use the heated tacking iron to tack the tissue to the back of the print on each of the four sides. The tissue must be the same size or larger than the print, and it must be the correct type for the paper you used to make the print.

Once the tissue is tacked to the print, you turn the print face up and trim off excess tissue—or even portions of the print if you wish to crop it—with a mat knife and a metal straightedge. Then, using a soft cloth to protect the print from fingerprints, you position the print backed with tissue on the mounting board and carefully lift the corners of the print to tack the tissue to the board.

You put a cover sheet over the print to protect it from the heating surface in the top of the press. You should never use newsprint or anything with printing on it as a cover sheet because the words will become imprinted on your print. Although you can purchase special cover sheets, a smooth, high-gloss butcher paper works well.

You place the assembled board, tissue, print, and cover sheet into the heated press. When you take it out of the press, you apply pressure to the cover sheet with a book or your hands so the edges won't curl up as it cools.

If you mounted your print on a large board to leave a border, you might find mounting tissue protruding from the edges of the print. This tissue can be removed if you are careful by using a straightedge and a small utility knife or razor blade. If you don't hold the straightedge down tightly, however, the blade may slip and cause you to cut into the print or the board and ruin your work. If you bleed-mounted the print, you use a mat knife to trim the board and print to be flush along all four edges.

• **With a household iron.** If you do not have a mounting press and tacking iron, you can mount your prints with a regular household flatiron. In this method, you set the control for synthetic fibers. When you tack the tissue to the back of the print, you can't press too hard or you will crease the print. Working on a hard, flat surface minimizes the danger of creases.

You trim the print and the tissue in the same manner as before and position the tissue, print, and cover sheet on the mounting board. Then you seal the print to the board by ironing it with light strokes.

You should iron the print from the center outward to avoid getting air bubbles between print and board. If you do get bubbles, you can try working them out by ironing. If that doesn't work, you can prick the print with a small needle to allow the air to escape, then iron over the surface. Mounting with a household iron always holds some risk of causing creases on the print. It's good insurance to make one or two backup prints—just in case.

• **Alternatives.** One alternative if you lack a dry mount press is to use one of the positionable **cold mount tissues** now available. Simple pressure, without heat, is enough to bond the print to its backing. The print can usually be lifted off and mounted again if mistakes are made. This type of tissue is more expensive than dry mount tissue, but surer to use in the absence of a press. Another alternative is to matte the print. This involves fastening the print to the back of a cardboard window. This method is preferable when the print is to be framed.

SIX

How to

Mount Prints

Step 1: Turn on the mounting press, and preheat it to between 180°F and 210°F to mount a print on RC paper. Then turn on the tacking iron to preheat it as well.

Step 2: Place the mounting board in the press for 30 seconds to remove moisture from it.

Step 3: With a soft cloth, clean the print, and make sure that everything else you use is free from dirt and dust. Any dirt particles will cause lumps in the mounted print that can't be removed.

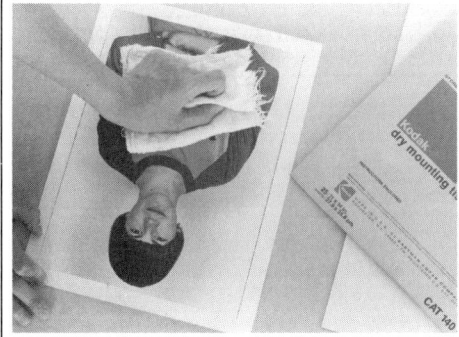

How to

Mount Prints

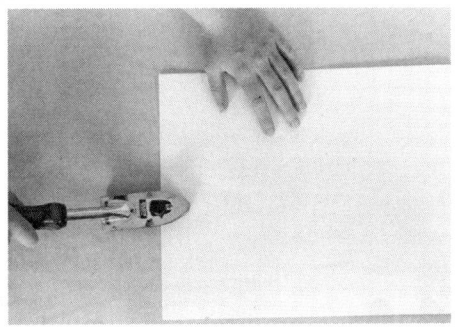

Step 4: Place the print face down on a clean, flat surface with the mounting tissue on top, and use the preheated tacking iron to tack the tissue to the print on all four sides.

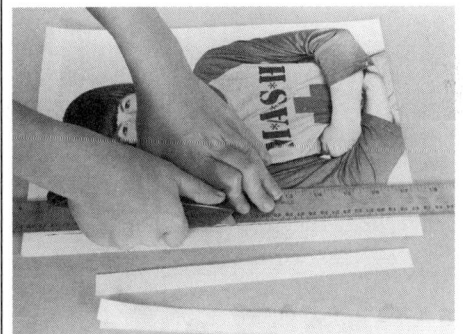

Step 5: Use the metal straightedge and the mat knife to trim the print and the tissue flush to size.

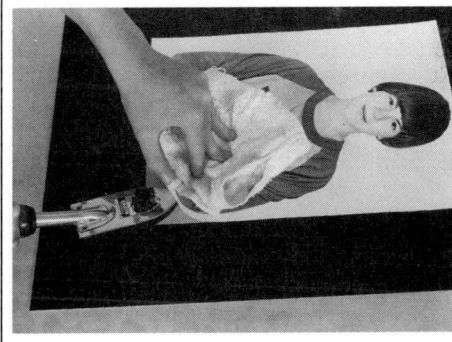

Step 6: Position the print and the tissue, face up, on the mounting board. Using a soft cloth to protect the print from fingerprints, carefully lift the corners of the print and tack the tissue to the board at the corners.

SIX

How to

Mount Prints

Step 7: Place the board, the tissue, the print, and the cover sheet into the heated press for 30 to 45 seconds.

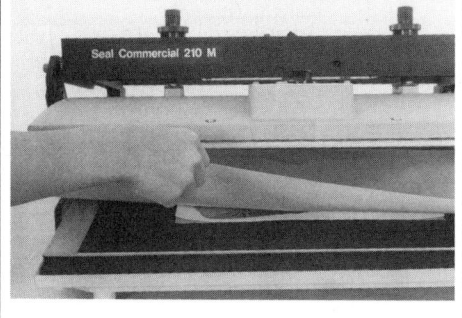

Step 8: Pull the mounted print out of the press, and apply pressure to the cover sheet so the edges don't curl up as it cools.

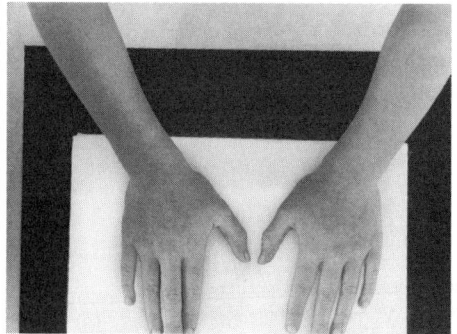

Step 9: If the print is to be bleed-mounted flush to the edges of the board, trim the board and print with the mat knife and straightedge.

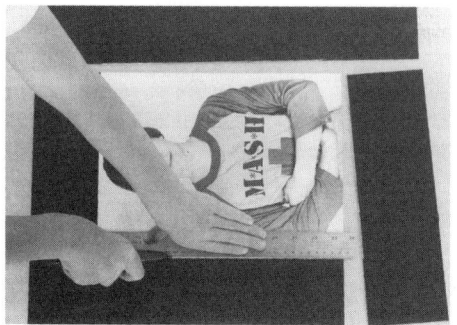

SIX

What Can
Go Wrong

Even experienced printers find that things do go wrong in the darkroom. Some problems just can't be avoided all of the time. Fortunately, there are things that you can do when, despite your best efforts, you have a problem print.

Problem 1:
White spots on print

White spots or scratches on the print.

Probable Cause:

You did not thoroughly clean the negative, or in the case of scratches, you did not handle the negative or wet print carefully enough.

Solution:

Make a new print being more careful, or use a photographic dye such as Spotone, to touch up the print you already have.

Problem 2 (A):
Black spots on print

Black spots or scratches on the print.

Probable Cause:

You may have deep nicks or scratches on the negative or pinholes caused by air bubbles on the film during development.

Solution (B):

Make a new print cropping away the damaged area on the negative, or use photographic bleach to lighten the dark spot or scratch.

A. Problem print

B. Solution print

What Can
Go Wrong

Problem 3 (A):
Part of image too dark

Probable Cause:

The area needed less exposure than the rest of the image.

Solution (B):

Dodge the area by using your hand or a dodging tool to limit the amount of light from the enlarger that it receives relative to the rest of the print.

A. Problem print

B. Solution print

Assembling a Portfolio

Now that you know how to take photographs and make prints, it is time to think about selling them. As a way to prepare for this step, it is important to put together a portfolio. A portfolio is the sheaf of mounted photos that you carry around with you to show prospective customers your worth as a photographer. Portfolios are very personal statements, so they vary greatly between individuals.

It is a good idea to have your portfolio ready at all times, updating it with new work from time to time. When you put your portfolio together, you'll want to keep certain basic points in mind.

Select only the best photographs for your portfolio. You shouldn't try to show how you have improved over the years. Don't feel the portfolio has to be large. Ten superb prints are better than a collection of 20 prints that includes one mediocre example of your work. It is only human nature that the photograph most likely to be remembered by a prospective employer will be the mediocre one.

Make good prints and mount them carefully. You can then place them in a large leather or cardboard folder that closes or ties for showing your photos one by one when you meet prospective clients. It is a good idea to identify the photos on the back.

Consider preparing several portfolios. If you take various kinds of photographs, it's a good idea to have more than one portfolio—for example, one for architecture and one for advertising.

Gather printed examples of how your photos were used. If you've had photographs published in annual reports, brochures, magazine articles, or the like, you can take tear sheets from the publications along in another folder when you meet prospective clients.

Prepare a portfolio on slides. You can easily send such a portfolio to potential clients out of town. This concise record of your work is less bulky and easier to ship than the portfolio you carry around with you. If possible, you should also prepare several "credit" slides that introduce your work ("The photographs of Jane Doe") along with your name, address, and telephone number.

Keep your portfolio updated and ready to show. Customers usually want a photographer on the day they call you and can't wait to make a decision while you spend a day in the darkroom making prints of your last three assignments.

Selling Your Photographs

The selling of photographs can consume a book longer than this one. The business side of photography is complicated and less rewarding than the enjoyable hours spent behind the camera or in the darkroom. If you want to become more than a "weekend photographer," however, you will need to know how to sell your photos.

You must first decide how serious you are about becoming a professional photographer or, at least, a good amateur who sells photos regularly. This decision will lead you in one of two directions.

The task of the amateur is relatively easy. Make contact with your local newspaper editor to find out that publication's photo needs. If the newspaper has no regular photographer, you might be able to take photos to illustrate travel articles or feature stories. If you want to go beyond that kind of occasional work to augment your income, you might want to take out an advertisement offering to do wedding shots, baby photos, or pictures for local clubs and organizations or school districts. This kind of photography is sometimes repetitious and, for the wedding, school, and baby portraits, requires that you buy special lighting equipment. It can be lucrative, however, especially in the repeat business that comes from school and wedding shots.

SIX

For the professional photographer wanting to branch out beyond the kind of local business noted above for the amateur, the way is more complicated. The best approach requires that you take yourself seriously as a photographer and set yourself up in business, just like you were opening a small store or going into business as a plumber. There are a number of things you can do to make the process a little easier.

Organize an office. Whether in your home or in a commercial office building, you should have an office complete with desk, files, and, most important of all, letterhead stationery, envelopes, business cards, and statements for billing customers. You will want to select a name and have a logo designed for your business. You can use that logo and name—set attractively in readable type—on the letterhead, envelopes, cards, and statements. Since you will be operating a small business, you may want to consult an accountant about bookkeeping and tax matters. You will need to keep records for income taxes and may have to collect sales taxes, as well as obtain a local resale license from your city and state tax boards.

Your potential customers needn't know that your office is at home in a room that is used to hold dust mops. The important thing is for you to look professional upon your first meeting. The quality of your photographs is more important, of course, but you may not get the chance to display your ability if your business operation looks sloppy and amateurish to an outsider.

Decide what kind of photographer you are and study the market for such photos carefully. The various kinds of photography will be discussed in Chapter 14. All of these segments include customers with special needs. You should study books like *Photographer's Market*, which tells what many magazines and newspapers around the country want in the way of photographs from freelancers. Other freelance assignment categories are detailed in such books as well. If you are aiming at a more local market—for example, advertising agencies, architects, or industrial firms—you can start calling on potential customers personally to make contacts and show your work. You can also consider feeding photographs to stock picture agencies as a supplement to your income. Such agencies, which are listed in *Photographer's Market*, collect photos on many subjects and sell them for various uses.

Prepare a brochure. It helps to have a brochure that details your capabilities and shows examples of your work. You can then mail the brochure to prospective clients or have it ready to leave behind after one of your personal visits.

Start taking the kind of pictures that fit the market you are trying to reach. Don't snap the camera shutter until you have put yourself in the shoes of a prospective client, whether that person be an advertising account executive, an architect, or a magazine photography director.

Try to sell the same photograph to several, non-competing markets. You can thus make your ideas pay off with only an initial investment of time and money.

File your negatives, contact sheets, and prints carefully. You will know where everything is quickly if you develop a good filing system (Figure 6.10). Selling your own photos from your stock is lucrative as is the selling of additional prints to a customer who hired you to take them initially. Your photos won't do you any good if you can't find the negatives when a call comes in.

Be prepared to move quickly to sell photos to national publications. When a major news event happens in your area, you must be able to assess the importance of the event instantly and to be there to take the pictures no one else can get. It helps to have contacted photo editors at national publications in a routine way beforehand. Luck plays a big part in this, of course, but you can let a good opportunity slip by if you don't know how to handle it. The photographer who took some of the first (and only) shots of the eruption of Mount St. Helens in 1980 (Figure 14.1) was a 23-year-old staffer on a nearby small daily newspaper who happened to be in the right place at the right time. His photos of the event have appeared in *Time*, *Life*, and several books.

Enter contests and brag about your awards. You can boast about your awards in your brochure and on your personal visits to clients. You can also set up displays of your work at local galleries, public buildings, or even shopping malls and department stores. All of this attracts attention to you and your work.

Set your prices carefully. You will want to make sure you do not give your work away, but you do not want to lose business either by charging too much. Photo organizations like the National Press Photographers Association can give you the standard rates in your area for certain kinds of photo work. Professionals usually charge a day rate plus expenses for assignment work and so much per print for sales of their own photos.

Never let your quality slip. When you get an assignment, you must take the time to shoot the job well, making sure you know in advance what the customer wants and then giving exactly what has been asked for. You must also take pains in the darkroom with printing and be sure to meet deadlines scrupulously.

Improve your photography. It is important to work constantly at improving your skills as a photographer. You can do this in a number of ways: by attending workshops and taking classes, by joining a local camera club, by visiting photo

SIX

FIGURE 6.10.
A ring binder file for organizing and storing negatives

exhibits. Good professional photographers are always striving to learn new and different techniques. The workshops have the additional advantage of allowing you to meet people, both noted professionals and others at your same skill level.

REVIEW
Questions

1. Why is contrast so important to a successful print?
2. What are contrast filters?
3. How do contrast filters improve a print?
4. What is cropping and how does it improve a print?
5. What techniques are used to crop a print?
6. What is "dodging" and how does it improve a print?
7. What is "burning" and how does it improve a print?
8. What is "bleaching" and when can it help a print?
9. How can spots—both black and white—be eliminated on a final print?
10. What techniques should be used in mounting finished prints?
11. What is a portfolio?
12. What are the main considerations in assembling a portfolio of work?
13. What are the best ways to sell your photographs?
14. How can a photographer set up an office?
15. Why is it important to study various photo markets?
16. Why is it important to file negatives, contact sheets, and prints carefully?
17. Why are contests important to the successful photographer?

Bibliography

"Hanging Bodies of the Four Conspirators" by Alexander Gardner, July 7, 1865

PRACTICE
BIBLIOGRAPHY
GLOSSARY

Bibliography

"Hanging Bodies of the Four Conspirators" by Alexander Gardner, July 7, 1865
(Courtesy of the Library of Congress)

One of Mathew Brady's best assistants was Alexander Gardner, who traveled far and wide to cover many major events of the Civil War. Gardner left Brady's employ in 1863 in anger over his boss' failure to give other photographers credit in a photo book. After photographing battles and leaders, Gardner took a series of shots of the four people tried for conspiring with John Wilkes Booth in the murder of President Abraham Lincoln. In this final frame, the hooded bodies of George Atzerodt, David E. Herold, Lewis Payne, and Mary E. Surratt are seen hanging from the scaffold at the Washington Arsenal on July 7, 1865. Gardner later published his own book of war photos in 1866 and went on to take memorable images of the American West.

History

Adams, Ansel. *Ansel Adams: An Autobiography* (Boston: Little, Brown, 1985)

Adams, Ansel, Mary Street Alinder, and Andrea Gray Stillman. *Ansel Adams: Letters & Images, 1916-1984* (Boston: Little, Brown, 1988)

Avedon, Richard. *An Autobiography* (New York: Random House, 1993)

Capa, Robert, Cornell Capa and Richard Whelan. *Robert Capa: Photographs* (New York: Alfred A. Knopf, 1985)

Cartier-Bresson, Henri. *Henri Cartier-Bresson* (New York: Aperture, 1987)

Coe, Brian. *The Birth of Photography: The Story of the Formative Years, 1800-1900* (London: Ash & Grant, 1976)

_____ . *George Eastman & the Early Photographers* (London: Priory Press, 1973)

Edward, Gary. *International Guide to 19th Century Photographers & Their Works* (New York: Macmillan, 1988)

Eisenstaedt, Alfred and Arthur A. Goldsmith. *The Eye of Eisenstaedt.* (New York: Viking Press, 1969)

Evans, Walker. *Walker Evans: American Photographs* (New York: Abrams, 1990)

Ford, Colin and Karl Steinorth. *You Press the Button, We Do the Rest: The Birth of the Snapshot* (London: Dick Nishen Publishing, 1988)

Galassi, Peter. *Henri Cartier-Bresson: The Early Work* (New York: Museum of Modern Art/New York Graphic Society, 1987)

Gernsheim, Helmut. *The History of Photography* (New York: McGraw-Hill, 1970)

_____ . *The Rise of Photography: The Age of Collodion* (London: Thames & Hodson, 1988)

International Museum of Photography and Robert Sobieszek. *Masterpieces of Photography from the George Eastman House* (New York: Abbeville Press, 1985)

Life: The First 50 Years (Boston: Little, Brown, 1986)

PRACTICE
BIBLIOGRAPHY
GLOSSARY

Lovell, Ronald P., Fred Zwahlen and James Folts. *Two Centuries of Shadow Catchers: A History of Photography* (Albany: Delmar Publishers, 1995)

Maloney, John F. *Vintage Cameras and Images: An Identification and Value Guide* (Florence, Alabama: Books Americana, 1981)

Newhall, Beaumont. *The History of Photography: From 1839 to the Present Day, 5th ed.* (New York: Museum of Modern Art, 1982)

_____ . *Supreme Instant: The Photography of Edward Weston* (Boston: Little, Brown, 1986)

Ohrn, Karin Becker. *Dorothea Lange & the Documentary Tradition* (Baton Rouge: Louisiana University Press, 1980)

Rosenblum, Naomi. *A World History of Photography* (New York: Abbeville Press, 1984)

Smith, W. Eugene and Ben Maddox. *Let Truth Be the Prejudice: W. Eugene Smith, His Life and Photographs* (New York: Aperture, 1985)

Weston, Edward. *The Daybooks of Edward Weston, Vol. I, Mexico, Vol. II, California* (Millerton, New York: Aperture, 1961)

Weston, Edward and Richard H. Cravens. *Edward Weston* (New York: Aperture, 1988)

Whelan, Richard. *Robert Capa: A Biography* (New York: Alfred A. Knopf, 1985)

Whelan, Richard. *Alfred Stieglitz: A Biography* (Boston: Little, Brown, 1995)

Photojournalism

Evans, Harold. *Pictures on a Page* (Belmont, California: Wadsworth, 1978)

Geraci, Philip. *Photojournalism: Making Pictures for Publication, 2nd ed.* (Dubuque, Iowa: Kendall/Hunt, 1976)

Johnson, Brooks. *Photography Speaks: 66 Photographers on Their Art* (New York: Aperture/The Chrysler Museum, 1989)

Mydans, Carl. *Carl Mydans: Photojournalist* (New York: Abrams, 1993)

Photography in General

Davis, Philip. *Photography, 7th ed.* (Brown & Benchmark, 1995)

Eastman Kodak Company Staff. *How to Take Good Pictures* (Saunders, 1990)

_____ . *The Joy of Photography, 3rd ed.* (New York: Addison Wesley, 1991)

Hedgecoe, John. *John Hedgecoe's Complete Guide to Black & White Photography* (Sterling, 1994)

Horenstein, Henry. *Black & White Photography: A Basic Manual, 2nd ed.* (Boston: Little, Brown, 1983)

Joseph, Michael and Dave Saunders. *The Complete Photography Course* (New York: Viking Penguin, 1994)

Life Library of Photography (New York: Time-Life Books, 1970-1975, 17 volumes)

London, Barbara and John Upton. *Photography, 5th ed.* (New York: HarperCollins, 1993)

Rosen, Marvin and David L. DeVries. *Introduction to Photography, 4th ed.* (Belmont, California: Wadsworth, 1993)

Sontag, Susan. *On Photography* (New York: Farrar, Strauss & Giroux, 1977)

Suess, Bernard J. *Mastering Black & White Photography* (Allworth Press, 1995)

Warren, Bruce. *Photography* (Los Angeles: West Publishing Company, 1993)

PRACTICE
BIBLIOGRAPHY
GLOSSARY

Equipment/Specific Techniques

Adams, Ansel. *Natural Light Photography* (Hastings-on-Hudson, New York: Morgan & Morgan, 1965)

_____ . *Artificial Light Photography* (Hastings-on-Hudson, New York: Morgan & Morgan, 1968)

_____ . *The Negative* (Hastings-on-Hudson, New York: Morgan & Morgan, 1968)

_____ . *The Print* (Hastings-on Hudson, New York: Morgan & Morgan, 1968)

_____ . *Camera and Lens* (Dobbs Ferry, New York: Morgan & Morgan, 1979)

Brown, Alan et al. *Lighting Secrets for the Professional Photographer* (Cincinnati, Ohio: Writers Digest, 1990)

Eastman Kodak Company Staff. *Existing-Light Photography* (Saunders Photo, 1991)

Freeman, Michael. *Film* (New York: Amphoto Books, 1988)

Gruen, Al. *Contact Sheet* (New York: Amphoto Books, 1982)

Herwig, Ellis. *The Handbook of Color Photography* (New York: Amphoto Books, 1982)

Hunter, Fit and Paul Fuqua. *Light, Science & Magic: An Introduction to Photographic Lighting* (Boston: Focal Press, 1990)

Kimber, David. *Lighting for Glamour Photography: A Complete Guide to Professional Techniques* (Watson-Guptill, 1994)

Pittaro, Ernest M., ed. *Photo Lab Index* (Dobbs Ferry, New York: Morgan & Morgan, published annually)

Selling Photographs

Brown, Nancy. *Photographing People for Stock: How to Take Pictures That Sell Again & Again* (New York: Amphoto Books, 1993)

Canavor, Natalie. *Sell Your Photographs: The Complete Marketing Strategy for the Freelancer* (Madrona Publishers, 1979)

Casewit, Curtis W. *Freelance Photography: Advice from the Pros* (New York: Macmillan, 1979)

Davis, Harold. *The Photographer's Publishing Handbook* (New York: Images NY, 1991)

Engh, Rohn. *Sell and Resell Your Photos* (Cincinnati, Ohio: Writers Digest, 1992)

Jacobs, Lou, Jr. *Selling Stock Photography: How to Market Your Photographs for Maximum Profit* (Watson-Guptill, 1992)

Photographer's Market (Cincinnati, Ohio: Writer's Digest, published annually)

Purcell, Ann and Carl Purcell. *Stock Photography: The Complete Guide* (Cincinnati, Ohio: Writers Digest, 1993)

Law and Photography

Berkeley, Adrian. *The Focal Guide to Photography and the Law* (Butterworth-Heinemann, 1993)

Duboff, Leonard. *The Photographer's Business & Legal Handbook* (New York: Images NY, 1989)

_____ . *The Law (in Plain English) for Photographers* (Allworth Press, 1995)

PRACTICE
BIBLIOGRAPHY
GLOSSARY

Glossary

Astronaut Edwin Aldrin Walking on the Moon by Neil Armstrong, July 20, 1969

Glossary

Astronaut Edwin Aldrin Walking on the Moon by Neil Armstrong, July 20, 1969
(Courtesy of the National Aeronautics and Space Administration)

Seconds before Neil Armstrong set foot on the surface of the moon, he pulled a lanyard that released a television camera from a compartment on the side of lunar module. In this way, he was able to share his historic walk with millions of viewers around the world. In 1.3 seconds, Armstrong's image appeared on TV sets everywhere.

Nineteen minutes later, his fellow astronaut, Edwin Aldrin, stepped onto the moon. They immediately set up another TV camera to give people a broader look at the Sea of Tranquillity, their landing site. They then unfurled a 3 ft. x 5 ft. American flag, stiffened by wire so it would seem to be flying on the windless lunar plain. In addition to setting up the TV cameras, Armstrong also snapped shots of the moon and Aldrin walking around. In this photo, Armstrong is seen reflected in Aldrin's visor as is the lunar module.

Explorers had carried cameras with them for much of photography's long history, but never to the surface of the moon—a place so distant and legendary. Photography, as well as mankind, had been part of something truly historic and revolutionary.

accent light: often a spotlight that is placed high above and to the rear of the subject.

activator: an ingredient in the developer that makes it alkaline. A strong alkali produces a rapid-acting developer and high contrast; a weak alkali gives a relatively slow-acting developer and less contrast.

additive primary: one of the three colors (red, green, or blue) that create white light when added together.

advertising photographer: a photographer who takes photographs of products or people that appear in advertisements.

agitation: turning the developing tank upside down and back so the developer flows freely and evenly over the entire surface of the film; rocking the developing tray gently back and forth so the developer flows evenly over a print.

ambient light: light that surrounds a subject to be photographed, usually continuous light as distinguished from light added by flash.

angle of view: the angle, or width of the scene in front of the camera, which is "seen" by the lens.

antihalation layer: the layer of film that keeps light rays from being reflected back up through the film and exposing it a second time.

aperture: the adjustable opening of a lens through which light passes; used to adjust the intensity (brightness or dimness) of the light.

aperture priority: an automatic exposure mode that permits you to set the aperture and select the depth of field; the camera will automatically set the shutter speed to give the correct exposure.

appropriation: a violation of a person's privacy rights by using the person's name or likeness for trade or advertising purposes without their permission.

architectural photographer: a photographer who makes a living taking photographs of buildings and building interiors.

artificial light: light added to a scene by the photographer—for example, floodlights or flash.

art photographer: a photographer whose photographs of people and objects are works of art like those created by a painter or a sculptor.

ASA (American Standards Association): the numerical rating indicating the light sensitivity of a particular type of film; replaced by ISO index in recent years.

autofocus lens: a lens that can be electronically focused by circuity built into the camera body.

automatic exposure: the feature on some cameras that automatically sets the aperture or shutter speed or both.

autowinder: a camera attachment that automatically advances the film and cocks the shutter after each exposure is made at a rate of about two frames per second; slower and less expensive than a motor drive.

average gray: 18% reflectance of the incident light, the same amount of light reflected by an average scene; the tone used to calibrate reflected light meters.

averaging meter: a through-the-lens metering system that measures and averages varying intensities of light and shadow areas electronically.

PRACTICE
BIBLIOGRAPHY
GLOSSARY

background light: light that shines solely on the background.

banding: abrupt transition from one gray level to another in a digital photograph.

bit: a binary digit. Can contain a value of 0 or 1.

bit depth: in a digital photograph, the amount of computer storage allotted to each pixel.

bleaching: lightening or removing areas of a print by applying chemical bleach and then fixing the print again.

bleed mount: a means of mounting a print that allows the photo to extend to all four edges of the board, with no border.

body: the housing for all the parts of the camera; designed to keep out light.

bounce light: light, usually from a flash that is indirectly bounced or reflected off a surface toward the subject. The light is thereby softened or made more diffuse.

bracketing: taking photos at several exposure settings to offer insurance against incorrect exposure and to experiment with exposure effects on the final negative or transparency.

brightness: the lightness or darkness of a color.

burning: manipulating a print in the darkroom to give one part of it additional exposure to darken it.

byte: a group of eight binary digits, or bits. Can contain values between 0 and 255.

cable release: a long, flexible wire with a plunger at one end and a socket at the other that attaches to the shutter release of the camera.

calotype: a photographic process developed by inventor William Henry Fox Talbot in 1835 that allowed him to make multiple copies of a positive image from a single "negative".

camera: a box-like device with a shutter that, when opened, admits light to enable an object to be focused by a lens on a photo-sensitive film or plate thereby producing a photographic image.

camera bags: made of canvas, leather, plastic, or aluminum, a camera bag both protects and makes transportable all photographic equipment and supplies.

camera cases: protects the camera, especially the lens, from damage, dust, and moisture.

camera obscura: the forerunner of the modern camera, a room with a single small opening to the outside in one wall. An inverted image of the outdoor scene was projected on the opposite wall.

can opener: a device used to open chemical containers and to pry open film cassettes.

cassette chamber: the part of the camera that holds the film cassette.

CCD: charge-coupled device; a sensor that converts light into an electrical signal.

center of interest: the focal point within a photograph, usually the subject.

center-weighted meter: a metering system that calculates exposure settings by operating through the lens. It bases the exposure more on light reaching the center of the viewfinder area than light at the frame edges.

charge-coupled device: a sensor that can convert light into an electronic signal: it captures the image in a still video camera in the way film does in a conventional camera.

chromogenic: a system for creating a color image by forming dyes in each emulsion layer of color film.

clamp tripod: an alternative to a full-size tripod. The clamp tripod is screwed into the tripod socket of the camera, then clamped to a firm surface.

CMYK color: color formation using the three subtractive primary colors (cyan, magenta, and yellow) plus a fourth neutral ("K") layer.

cold mount tissue: a thin paper used for mounting a print; simple pressure, without heat, is enough to bond the print to its backing.

color balance: a match between the color sensitivity of color film and the color of the light source.

color complements: colors opposite one another on the color wheel.

color gamut: the range of colors produced by a color system.

color wheel: a diagram showing the relationship between the additive and subtractive primaries.

commercial photographer: a photographer who operates a studio and/or laboratory and takes pictures to sell to the public.

compression ratio: the amount of reduction in file size produced by a compression approach.

contact sheet: a proof print of every frame on a roll of film; so named because the negative and photographic paper are in direct contact when made.

continuous light: a steady source of light, such as light bulbs or floodlights; as distinct from flash or strobe light.

contrast: the range of tones in a negative or print; the difference in extremes between light tones (highlights) and dark tones (shadows).

contrast filter: in taking pictures, a colored filter used to control the tonal rendition of colored objects on black-and-white film; often used to darken the sky so clouds stand out; in enlarging, a plastic filter used to control the contrast of blacks and whites in the finished print.

contrast grade: the contrast characteristics of a particular batch of enlarging paper. For example, a number 2 grade paper is considered normal contrast.

contrasty print: a print with exaggerated differences between light and dark tones.

copyright: the exclusive right to reproduce, publish, and sell the matter and form of a literary or artistic work.

copyright notice: a legal phrase displayed on material giving notice that the material is protected by copyright law.

copyright registration: a procedure for establishing and maintaining copyright claims, made through the Copyright Office of the Library of Congress in Washington, D.C.

correction filter: used to compensate for differences between the color sensitivity of a certain type of film and the type (color) of light used to expose it.

crop marks: marks made to indicate the part of the frame to be used.

cropping: selecting the portion of a frame of film to be printed in an enlargement.

darkroom: a room in which illumination can be controlled or eliminated so that photographic material can be processed.

PRACTICE
BIBLIOGRAPHY
GLOSSARY

daguerreotypes: In 1839, painter Louis Daguerre discovered by accident that he could produce a positive image by sensitizing a silver-plated metal sheet with iodine fumes, exposing it to light, developing it over mercury fumes, and then fixing the image in a salt solution. He called the resulting images daguerreotypes.

daylight film: used with daylight, whether outdoors or coming indoors through a window or skylight.

density: the opacity ("blackness") of an area in a film or print image.

depth of field: the zone in front of, and behind, the subject that is acceptably sharp.

developer: a chemical solution that makes the latent image on film or photographic paper visible by converting exposed silver halide crystals to metallic silver.

developing agent: an ingredient in film or paper developer that converts exposed silver halide crystals to the metallic silver that forms the image.

developing tank: a processing tank made of plastic or metal in which film is placed for developing.

diffusion: to scatter light so it is less directional and casts less distinct shadows.

direction: the angle at which light strikes a subject, a factor that affects the way texture and shape are depicted in the photograph.

dodging: manipulating a print in the darkroom to give one part of it less exposure and thus lighten it.

dryer: a machine for drying film or prints after they have been processed.

dry mounting: a means of attaching prints to a cardboard backing for more permanence and easy display through use of a heated press, an iron, and special adhesive tissue.

dry mount tissue: a thin paper coated with adhesive that gets sticky when heated; the tissue holds the photographic print to the mounting board.

dusting equipment: soft brushes used to remove dust and pieces of lint from negatives and from the enlarger lens.

DX-coated film: film cassettes that are printed with a pattern of black and silver squares which represent the film's ISO index.

dye-destruction system: a system for creating a color image by beginning with a full set of dyes and then removing those that are not needed in the image.

dye-incorporated system: a system in which potential dyes are included in color film during manufacture and are converted to visible dyes during processing.

dye-injection system: a system in which dyes are introduced into each emulsion layer of color film during development. The layers are developed and dyed one at a time.

easel: a fixed or adjustable frame placed on the baseboard of an enlarger to hold the paper flat for exposure.

electronic darkroom: a computer used to make photographs electronically without the need to develop negatives and print them conventionally.

emulsion: the photographically active layer of film or paper containing silver halide crystals suspended in gelatin.

enlarger: a piece of equipment used to project an image from a negative to a sheet of photographic paper to make prints of a size larger than the original negative.

enlarging: the process of making an enlarged photographic positive image from a negative.

exclusive rights: under copyright law, the owners of literary or artistic work have five basic rights: 1) right to reproduce the work, 2) right to prepare derivative works (second editions or translations), 3) right to distribute the work to the public, 4) right of public performance, and 5) right of public display of the work. Only these owners have such rights exclusively.

existing light: light already existing at the scene to be photographed; usually distinguished from natural or artificial light.

exposure value: the value that can be used by photographers to refer to the group of all the shutter speed-aperture combinations that give correct exposure with a certain brightness level.

false light: a violation of a person's privacy rights by using the person's name or likeness in a fictionalized or semifictionalized account so as to give a false impression.

fashion photographer: a photographer who takes pictures of models wearing different kinds of clothes for use in fashion magazines and advertising.

fast: a type of film or paper that is very sensitive to light; a lens with a large maximum aperture for its focal length (e.g., a f/2.8 200 mm lens).

fiber-based paper: "conventional" photographic paper; an emulsion coated onto paper that is durable when wet.

file: a computer stores each image as a separate collection of numbers, call a file. File sizes are commonly given in kilobytes or megabytes.

fill flash: artificial light directed at subjects to fill or lighten shadow areas usually created by strong sunlight.

fill light: the light that is used to fill in and soften the shadows created by the main light when using artificial light.

film-advancing mechanism: moves the film from left to right in order to expose as many pictures as are on the strip of film.

film base: the acetate or polyester layer of film on which the other layers rest.

film clips: devices that hold film for drying.

film development time: the amount of time film is exposed to developer.

film-holding mechanism: the part of the camera that holds film at the focal plane.

film recorder: can print a computer-processed image on conventional color film or paper.

filter: a tinted or colored piece of optical glass, plastic, or gelatin attached to the lens of a camera to modify light before it reaches the film.

filter factor: a multiplying number that serves to compensate for the absorption of radiant energy (light) by a filter.

fish-eye lens: an extreme wide-angle lens, usually with a focal length of 8 mm or less and characterized by a circular image.

fixer: the chemical that renders a photographic image stable on film or print.

fixing: making a photographic image stable by removing unexposed silver halide crystals from the emulsion.

flash: a brief burst of high intensity light, synchronized with the shutter opening of the camera.

flat print: a print that lacks contrast—that is, it has no dark blacks or clear whites.

floodlight: a light source that spreads its illumination over a wide area.

focal length: the distance between the lens and the plane of focus when the lens is focused at infinity.

focal plane shutter: a shutter built into the camera body just in front of the film plane, or plane of focus, made of two overlapping curtains forming an adjustable window.

focusing mechanism: the part of the camera that moves the lens toward or away from the subject to be photographed, and toward or away from the film upon which the image will be recorded.

focusing screen: a piece of etched glass used to view and focus upon the scene in front of the camera.

frame: one of a succession of pictures on a strip of film.

framing: selecting a portion of the scene in front of the camera to be contained in the viewfinder frame; also, using a natural frame (window, arch, tree branch, etc.) as an element in composing a photograph.

freelance photographer: a photographer who is self-employed, works independently, and is generally hired to do specific jobs, from portraiture to news photography.

fresnel lens: a focusing aid with concentric line patterns that is used to brighten the outer edges of the screen.

f-stop: a numerical indicator of the size of the aperture; the larger the f-number, the smaller the physical lens opening.

gelatin supercoating: a light-sensitive emulsion containing silver halide crystals, and a paper base that protects the emulsion from scratches.

grain magnifier: an optical device that helps focus the image from an enlarger.

gray card: a card that is gray in color (one having 18 percent reflectance) used to achieve the "average gray" standard needed for photography; made by Kodak and called the Kodak Neutral Test Card.

gray scale: in any photograph, conventional or digital, the patterns of gray tones that are produced by the direct action of light.

ground-glass system: a focusing system wherein light from the lens is projected onto a viewing screen.

guide number: used to calculate flash exposures; the product of the aperture and the flash-to-subject distance that gives correct exposure.

halftoning factor: the oversampling factor used in making digital scans that will later be printed using halftone dots.

heliography: a process developed by French physicist Joseph Niepce in 1816 that produced a positive copy of an engraving by exposing a glass plate coated with an asphalt-like substance.

high contrast film: black-and-white film that combines very high contrast with extremely high resolution and virtually microscopic grain.

highlights: the light areas in the original scene that appear on the negative as the relatively dense or opaque areas.

HSB color: a color model that allows control of hue, saturation, and brightness independently.

hue: the color itself, for example, red or blue or green.

hypo clearing agent: a solution that speeds the removal of fixer during the wash, thus reducing wash times.

imagesetter: typesetting machines capable of printing computer-processed images with a relatively high resolution.

incident light meter: an exposure meter that measures the intensity of light striking the subject.

industrial photographer: a photographer who works for a large corporation to take pictures of its products and personnel.

infrared film: black-and-white and color film possessing sensitivity in the infrared portion of the spectrum as well as in the visible region; ideal for experimental photos.

ink jet printer: squirts colored inks onto paper to print a computer-processed image.

intensity: the brightness or dimness of light.

intrusion: a violation of the privacy rights of another person when they have a reasonable expectation of privacy; for example, by using an extremely long telephoto lens or a concealed recording device. Invasion of privacy: a violation of the right of someone to be left alone. See appropriation, false light, intrusion, and publication of private matters.

ISO index: a numerical rating indicating the light sensitivity, or speed, of a particular type of film; replaced the ASA rating in name, although the rating values are interchangeable.

Lab color: a mathematically precise model for color representation that breaks each color into three components—*L*, *a*, and *b*.

laser printer: can print computer-processed images, but with relatively low resolution.

latent image: an image recorded in a light-sensitive emulsion upon exposure, but invisible; must be developed to become visible.

law enforcement photographer: a photographer who works for police and sheriffs' departments to take photos of crime scenes and homicide victims.

law of reciprocity: the photographic principle that you can interchange shutter speeds and aperture settings without changing overall exposure. For example, f/5.6 at 1/60 is the exposure equivalent of f/8 at 1/30.

leaf shutter: a shutter built into the lens consisting of several small overlapping spring-powered metal blades.

lens: the part of the camera that views the subject to be photographed and projects it onto the film as a completely reversed image; the part of the enlarger that projects a flat image (the negative) onto a flat plane (the enlarger baseboard).

lenshood: a detachable camera accessory that shields the lens from extraneous light.

libel: defamation, or holding someone up to ridicule, by written or printed words or pictures.

licensing agreement: a contract between a photographer and a second party to use a photograph for a specific purpose.

light-sensitive emulsion: in printmaking, light-sensitive emulsion is exposed to light and silver ions in the silver halide crystals are converted to metallic silver atoms to make a latent image.

PRACTICE
BIBLIOGRAPHY
GLOSSARY

line-conversion: a gray scale image is converted into an image that has no intermediate grays.

lossless compression: a method of making computer files smaller without losing any data.

lossy compression: a method of making computer files smaller where subtle information is sacrificed.

l-shaped croppers: cardboard guides that "frame" a contact sheet image before printing.

macro lens: a lens that enables a photographer to take pictures very close to the subject. A true macro lens permits shooting so close that the negative image is the same size as the original subject.

magnification: the size of the image on the film or final print relative to the original subject or negative.

main light: the major artificial light source used to illuminate a scene; used to create the primary shadowing on the subject; also called the key light.

manual exposure: the ability to vary camera aperture and shutter speed manually until the meter indicates correct exposure.

merger: a confusing association of subject with background.

microprism grid: a focusing spot that consists of many tiny prisms that break up, or exaggerate the blur of, an out-of-focus image. When focused, the image is clear and intact.

model release: a standardized form in which the person signing gives his or her consent to have the photograph taken and used by the photographer.

monopod: a one-legged stand for holding the camera.

motor drive: a camera attachment that automatically advances the film and cocks the shutter after each exposure; operates at the rate of about five frames per second. Mounting: the process of attaching a print to a cardboard backing. See dry mount and wet mount.

"M" synchronization: the designation for "medium peak" flash bulbs, camera synchronization for use with regular wire-filled flash bulbs.

natural light: a term photographers use to refer to light found outdoors in nature. (Strictly speaking, of course, all light is natural; or at least none is unnatural.)

negative: the developed image in which the light and dark tones of a photograph are reversed.

negative carrier: a frame for holding the negative inside an enlarger for printing.

negative sleeves: cellophane or plastic holders that protect negatives from damage.

neutral density filter: a filter that cuts down on the brightness of a scene, but it is "neutral" in that it does not alter color rendition.

normal lens: a lens with a focal length of approximately the same length as the diagonal measurement of the film format used (50 mm for 35 mm film).

overexposure: the result when too much light reaches the film or paper; causes a denser than normal negative or print. Panchromatic: film that is sensitive to the wavelengths from all colors of the visible spectrum.

panchromatic: film that is sensitive to the light of all colors as those seen by the human eye.

panning: moving the camera with a moving subject. The background will blur, but the subject should be relatively sharp.

paper base: the support for the gelatin supercoating and light-sensitive emulsion in photographic paper.

paper developer: a chemical used to bring out the visible images on photographic paper.

paper grade: see contrast grade.

paper safe: a special box designed to keep photographic paper from being exposed to light.

paper weight: the thickness of photographic paper: single or double for fiber-based paper; medium weight for resin-coated paper.

parallax effect: the difference between what is seen through the viewfinder of the camera and what is recorded on film due to the distance between the viewfinder and the lens; also called parallax error.

photoflood: an incandescent light bulb of high efficiency but limited life that works well to light interior scenes and portrait subjects.

photographic paper: a sensitized paper designed for use in making photographic prints.

photojournalism: a career in which a photographer uses a camera, in much the way a reporter uses a pencil, to record news events for newspapers and magazines.

pixel: picture element; a small cell, a component of a larger image, that may vary in tone from black through various shades of gray to white.

plane of focus: the hypothetical flat surface in image space that represents the focus of a distant flat object surface perpendicular to the lens.

polarizing filter: used to cut out polarized light primarily to eliminate reflections or to increase cloud contrast.

portfolio: a sheaf of mounted photos that a photographer uses to display his or her work for prospective customers.

portraits: photographs of people, usually of their faces.

posterization: an image that is composed of only a few distinct gray values.

preservative: an ingredient (usually sodium sulfite) in developer or fixer that prevents or retards spoiling and thus prolongs the life of these solutions.

pressure plate: a part of the film holding mechanism of a camera that keeps the film flat against the shutter.

privacy: the legal right to be left alone.

process color: the subtractive system used in graphic arts for printing full-color.

programmed exposure: an automatic exposure mode that sets both shutter speed and aperture.

proper contrast: a print with proper contrast contains a solid black, a bright white, and a full range of tones between.

publication of private matters: violation of a person's privacy rights by revealing private, intimate details about a person that others have no right to know.

pushing film: the technique for compensating for known underexposure of film with special development, often by prolonging development or using a high-energy developer.

push processing: giving extra development to a film to make up for loss of contrast that comes from underexposure.

rangefinder system: a focusing system that allows the photographer to see two images— a direct image through the viewfinder and a reflected image from a mirror.

reel: a spool or frame upon which exposed film is wound for developing.

reflected light meter: a meter that measures the light reflected from, or produced by, a subject to be photographed.

reflectors: a surface that reflects light toward the subject; usually used to throw light into shadow areas and increase shadow detail. Resin-coated paper: photographic paper that has been coated with a water-resistant plastic to allow faster processing, washing, and drying.

resin-coated paper: one type of photographic paper. The paper base has a top coating as well as a subcoating, both of which are water-resistant plastic and thus prevent chemicals from seeping into the paper base during processing.

resolution: the ability to resolve fine detail in a film, lens, or electronic imaging device.

restrainer: a chemical that holds back developer action, thus keeping fogging of film or paper at an acceptable level.

rewind knob: the foldable crank of the camera that rewinds film back into the magazine.

RGB color: color formation using the three additive primary colors, red, green, and blue.

rule of thirds: a rule of thumb for composition that entails dividing the frame into thirds horizontally and vertically to form four intersection points at which the subject can be effectively positioned.

safelight: a darkroom light with a built-in filter that screens out rays harmful to film or paper.

saturated colors: slight underexposure creates more intense, more saturated colors. Because many photographers want saturated colors, they routinely underexpose slide film by inflating the ISO speed rating by one-third stop.

saturation: the purity of a color; whether it tends to be grayish neutral or pure color.

scanner: a device for exposing an image on film by tracing light along a series of many closely spaced parallel lines; both film scanners and print scanners capture visual images in electronic form.

scissors: used to cut the leader off the film before winding it on the developing reel.

scratch-resistant substance: a coating of hard gelatin applied to the film to help protect it from abrasion.

shadows: the dark areas in the original scene depicted in the negative as relatively thin or transparent areas.

shutter: the gate-like mechanism that controls access of light to the film.

shutter curtain: the part of a focal plane shutter that moves across the film plane to expose it.

shutter priority: an automatic exposure mode that permits you to set the shutter speed to capture the subject at either a high speed or to show movement of the subject at a slower speed; the camera will automatically set the aperture to give the correct exposure.

silver salt/silver halide crystals: light-sensitive compounds used in photographic emulsions to record the image.

single-lens reflex: a camera design that uses a mirror system to allow the photographer to view the scene through the lens.

skylight filter: a filter intended to warm the slightly bluish shadows often encountered with color film, but often used simply for lens protection.

slow: a type of film that has low sensitivity to light; a lens with a relatively small maximum aperture for its focal length (an f/3.5 50 mm, for instance).

special-purpose lenses: lenses used for close-up work, technical or scientific photos, or architectural photos.

speed: a particular setting for the camera shutter; the light sensitivity of photographic materials as measured by the ISO or ASA of film of the ANSI rating for paper; the relative size of the maximum aperture for a lens of given focal length. See fast and slow.

split-image rangefinder prism assembly: the rangefinder focusing spot consists of two small prisms that cause an out-of-focus image to appear split in half in the viewfinder. Focusing brings the two halves together to form a whole image.

spotlight: a light that concentrates its output on a relatively small area of the subject.

spot meter: a meter that measures a small portion of the light reflected from a subject.

spotting: using dye to fill in and thus eliminate a dust spot or scratch on a print.

sprocket wheel: a device in the camera that engages the edge of the film and pulls it through the camera.

squeegee: a device to help remove excess water from film or prints before drying them.

stop bath: a chemical solution that stops the action of the developer by neutralizing it for both film and paper.

straight print: an unmanipulated enlargement made at a single exposure time.

strobe: an electronic flash unit that puts out a powerful, extremely brief burst of light.

subtractive primary: one of the three colors (yellow, magenta, cyan) used in photography and graphic arts printing to produce full-color images.

synchronization: coordination between the peak of flash light and the opening of the camera shutter so the flash output is used most effectively to expose the film. Tacking iron: an iron used in dry mounting prints.

table-top tripod: an alternative to a full-size tripod, a table-top tripod is small enough to fit into a camera bag.

take-up reel: the part of the camera that winds up film after it has been exposed.

telephoto lens: a lens of longer-than-normal focal length that magnifies objects.

test print: a contact print or enlargement containing trial exposure times.

test strip: a contact print containing trial exposure times done on part of a piece of photo paper.

thermal printer: uses heat to transfer dyes from a color ribbon to a receiver sheet to produce a full-color image of photographic quality from a computer-processed image. Also called thermal-dye transfer or dye-sublimation printer.

thermometer: an instrument used for gauging the temperature of chemicals used in the darkroom to process photographs.

timer: a darkroom clock with a sweep second hand that times enlarger exposure and development.

tongs: metal, plastic, or wooden devices used to move prints through trays of chemicals without getting fingers in the chemicals.

toning: using chemicals called toners to alter the tint or color of the silver image of a black-and-white print.

trays: shallow rectangular containers of metal or plastic in which prints are processed.

tri-pack construction: color film with three emulsion layers, one for each subtractive primary, coated onto a single film base.

tripod: a free-standing three-legged support for a camera.

tungsten film: used with light bulbs or photoflood lamps.

twin-lens reflex: a camera with one lens to focus light on the film and another to focus light on the viewing screen via a mirror.

ultraviolet filter: a filter intended to remove ultraviolet light and eliminate a secondary "ghost" image, but often used simply for lens protection.

underexposure: the result when too little light reaches the film or paper; causes a thinner-than-normal negative or a lighter-than-normal print.

variable contrast paper: photographic paper that allows control of contrast on the same paper through use of filters.

view camera: a camera design, the oldest in existence, in which the lens is separated from the film plane by an adjustable bellows.

viewfinder: the part of the camera that allows a photographer to see the subject to be photographed; a type of camera in which the light from the object to be photographed travels through the viewfinder to the eye, and separately through the lens to the film.

viewfinder attachments: augment the regular viewfinder of a camera when a tripod is used or to give a better look at scenes from waist-level, from above, from awkward angles, or to give a magnified view.

visible image: an image that has been developed.

wet collodion: a negative material consisting of a glass plate coated with a mixture of cellulose nitrate and potassium iodide and sensitized with silver nitrate. Developed in 1851, it all but replaced the previous processes. It was as sharp as the daguerreotype but also reproducible in the same way as the calotype in that it was a negative-positive process.

wet mounting: the use of a paste-like substance to mount large size prints to a cardboard or wooden backing, normally done when a print is too large to be dry mounted. See dry mount.

wetting agent: a chemical that promotes even film drying when it is added to the final processing rinse.

wide-angle lens: a lens of shorter-than-normal focal length that offers a wide angle of view.

work-made-for-hire agreement: an agreement between a photographer and a customer which gives ownership of resultant photographs to that customer, not the photographer.

"X" synchronization: the camera setting to be used with electronic flash.

zoom lens: a lens of variable focal length.

HANDBOOK OF PHOTOGRAPHY

Index